GO
PREACH!

A Primer for Beginning Preachers

John P. Gilbert

DISCIPLESHIP RESOURCES

PO BOX 340003 • NASHVILLE, TN 37203-0003

www.discipleshipresources.org

"Bible Commentary" — get one.

Cover and book design by Nanci H. Lamar
Edited by Linda R. Whited and Heidi L. Hewitt

ISBN 0-88177-384-0
Library of Congress Control Number 2002103141

DR384

CONTENTS

INTRODUCTION

Welcome to an exciting adventure. Preaching is one of the most rewarding, exhilarating, and difficult things you will ever be called on to do. And God has called you to preach.

This book will not make you a great preacher, since this book is a primer, a basic nuts-and-bolts beginning book on preaching. It is your first exposure to trying to write and deliver a sermon. It is not the end of the road toward preaching, but it is the tentative first step.

If you have preached dozens and dozens of sermons already, you may find this book simplistic. However, you will still find many valuable suggestions and ideas.

If you have never preached a sermon, you may find this book daunting. That's because it describes a long, detailed, involved process that will equip you to preach. Your first thought might be, *I can't do all of that. I don't have the time.* But the "that" about which you are speaking is the prayerful, conscientiousness preparation that goes into sermon construction. If you don't have time for that preparation, perhaps you ought to reconsider your call to preach. Maybe God is calling you to live out your discipleship in some other way.

So, read this primer as a recipe book or as a formula to get you started in sermon development and delivery. But just as you did not stop reading when you finished that first-grade reading primer ("Run, Spot, run!"), please do not stop reading and studying preaching with this primer.

Dozens of people in small-membership congregations in Massachusetts and Tennessee tolerated my initial efforts in preaching and wisely counseled me in love so that my proclamation of the gospel of Jesus Christ could become more effective. I thank them.

Go preach!

Jack Gilbert

1

GO PREACH!

Preaching's History, Theology, and Call

Remember the first time the thought came to you? You didn't think much of it at the time, but the thought, once planted, started to sprout. Maybe it sprouted just a little at first, but it soon became a nagging, growing feeling. It was that thought, that feeling, you had while you were sitting in church listening to the preacher. Or that thought, that feeling, you had on the way home from church one morning.

It was that thought, that feeling, that you had something to say, or that you would have taken the preacher's sermon in a different direction, or the feeling deep within you that said, "Why didn't the preacher make this point?" Or maybe it was the thought that you could do a better job at preaching.

If you had that last feeling, you quickly squashed it. You shouldn't criticize the preacher or claim to be able to preach better than she or he preaches. What about Christian humility?

But when that thought, that thought that you could preach, crept in (almost unwanted), it just stayed there, didn't it? You found yourself listening to sermons with a new interest. However, your interest was not just in hearing what the preacher had to say but in thinking about the ways you would preach that sermon or discuss that biblical text.

Once that thought gets planted, it stays there; and nothing you or I can do will drive it away. Why? Because it's the call: God's call to preach!

God calls all of us to many and varied tasks. Some are called to teach in the Sunday school, others to sing in the choir. Some are called to work with the homeless, others to carry out an intensive prayer ministry from their own homes. Each of us is a disciple of Jesus Christ. When we accept the forgiveness and new life that Christ offers, we accept the call to discipleship that comes with that call. Discipleship is not an option. Each of us is called to be a disciple and fully equipped for the unique and individual ministry to which God calls us.

Now, all of this means one thing: Those who are called to preach are no better (or worse) than anyone else. The call to preach is a ministry for which God has equipped some, just as the call to work in the physical healing arts is a ministry for which God has called others. Sometimes those who are called to preach think they are just a bit better or more righteous than others. What a perversion of the understanding of God's call. Paul put a quick stop to that kind of thinking in I Corinthians 12 and in Ephesians 4:11-12.

God's call to preach comes in a wide variety of ways and forms—some of them serious, some of them humorous, some of them almost shocking. But it's God's call; and once you hear that call, you have no way to turn back.

Remember Amos? He identified himself as nothing but a shepherd and a "dresser of sycamore trees" (whatever that is; scholars still aren't quite sure what he did). He claimed that once the lion roars, we cannot ignore it; once God calls us to preach, we cannot run from it. (Read Amos 7:12-15 and 3:3-8, especially verse 8.)

You have this book in your hand right now because you have been called to preach. Maybe you haven't been called to be a full-time pastor of a congregation or a world-famous pulpiteer, but you have been called to preach. Praise be to God!

Go Preach!

The title of this chapter, and indeed of this book, comes from a chapter in a book by M.A.C. Warren titled *The Christian Imperative*. I have no idea where or how I came across that book many years ago, but I know it changed my life. I had been struggling with an unclear sense of call to the ministry for many years. In fact, I got a four-year degree in a field as far removed from ministry as I could imagine so that I could ignore that call. I wandered for a year after college and then went into the armed forces for a couple years. (That was back in the days when the armed forces drafted young men for two years.) It was not until I was in the Army that the meaning of that word (*imperative*) in Warren's title hit me like a sledge hammer. An imperative is a directive or order, a command and a demand. You and I cannot ignore or deny an imperative placed on us.

The imperative placed on me, and the imperative (the demand) you are feeling that brought you to this place, is to go preach: to proclaim the gospel of Jesus Christ, to tell others of the great good news, or, as an old definition of evangelism says, to be a beggar who tells another beggar where to find bread.

But if you're anything like I was (and like Moses was in the third and fourth chapters of Exodus), your first response is, "Who? Me? I don't know the first thing about preaching."

Well, that's what this book is about. It's about the first things about preaching. It's not the end of your study of preaching but the beginning, the start, the primer. Reading this book won't make you a great preacher, but it will give you some hints and clues as to how to get started and where to turn for more help.

You'll want to look at the bibliography in the back of this book, for it contains a number of good books on preaching. Read widely and deeply on the subject of preaching. None of us is a born preacher, for we all need to develop and hone our skills continually. Look at the Scriptures. Jesus prepared for his ministry with his time in the wilderness, as did Paul. The apostles prepared long and hard for their ministry by living with the resurrected Christ for fifty days. These were days of preparation for them. As Jesus had taught them during the three years he was with them, so now did he fix those lessons within them before his ascension. A true preacher never stops reading, studying, evaluating her or his own sermons; nor does he or she stop listening to the sermons of others. A true preacher never stops improving and developing his or her skills. After all, this is part of what sanctifying grace is all about—going on to perfection. Make a commitment right now to read regularly from the books in the bibliography at the end of this book or from books recommended to you by your pastor and others whose opinions you value.

So, let's set out on an adventure. You bring that uncertain call to preach that you're feeling, and I'll bring many years of experience preaching in small-membership congregations. Together, we can learn something about preaching the gospel of Jesus Christ to a hungry, lonely, empty world.

It's Nothing New

Preaching is as old as time itself. Preaching began when humankind first learned to speak. (But let's not get into arcane anthropological debates about when and how that was.) Why? Because the spoken word preceded the written word by many centuries. For a long, long time in human history, the best way, indeed about the only way, to communicate was through spoken words with gestures. When one of our ancient ancestors had something to say to many of his or her sisters or brothers, that ancestor stood up and said it loud and clear—and perhaps preaching began.

But preaching is a particular kind of spoken communication. It's not directed at how to make a fire or to kill a buffalo; it's not designed to find gold or to plant crops. Its intent is not to sell a product or to make a deal.

• Preaching is the proclamation of good news.
• Preaching is the proclamation of the word God gives us to speak.
• Preaching is God's word uttered through human vessels.

The prophets knew what preaching is; that's why they began so many of their statements with, "Thus saith the Lord." In fact, the prophets of the Old Testament were not people who foretold the future; they were people who said what God told them to say, who uttered the words God had placed within them to proclaim to the community. Prophets were people who spoke the words God gave them to speak, just as contemporary preachers do.

The Old Testament is filled with eloquent preachers, people who announced what God had told them to say. Moses and Aaron; Deborah; the psalmists; the prophets, such as Isaiah, Huldah, Jeremiah, and Amos; Esther; and Koheleth (the preacher who wrote Ecclesiastes) are just a few of them.

Think of the New Testament: John the Baptist, Peter, Lydia, Paul, Philip. The list goes on and on.

Any list of preachers is crowned by the simple man who preached the Sermon on the Mount and the sermon in John, chapters 14 through 17, and whose sermons were spiced with stories of everyday people doing everyday things. (We call those stories the parables.) Along with all else that he was, Jesus was a preacher. With the exception of the story of Jesus writing in the dust of the ground (John 8), we have no biblical record of Jesus ever writing anything. He spoke and preached, and his preaching (and his life, death, and resurrection) transformed the entire universe.

The New Testament preachers became the models for the preachers of the early church and down through the centuries. Their names are legion: Augustine of Hippo and John Chrysostom (his name means golden mouth) of the early church, Martin Luther and John Calvin at the time of the Reformation, John Wesley and George Whitfield at the beginning of the Methodist movement, Jonathan Edwards and Cotton Mather in the Great Awakening in the American colonies, the circuit riders on the frontier of a growing America, Billy Sunday and Billy Graham during contemporary times. The list is endless.

Many of these preachers labored at a time when women were not allowed or expected to preach publicly. But we know both directly and indirectly that, throughout the centuries of Christianity, women have proclaimed the gospel in a wide variety of ways and left their mark on the proclamation of the gospel as surely as have the men. Indeed, the first Easter sermon was preached by women on their return from the empty tomb. That is just one of what could be countless examples. Fanny Crosby, who was blind, wrote somewhere between 5,500 and 9,000 hymns (she used many different names out of a sense of humility), and her hymns are still being sung in churches all across our land every week.

Through spoken word or music, all of these preachers—New Testament, early church, Reformation, contemporary—shared common characteristics, characteristics that still mark our preaching today:

- Preaching is the proclamation of the good news of Jesus Christ.
- Preaching is not the cataloging of another's sins unless accompanied by the good news of forgiveness and reconciliation with God.

- Preaching is a judgment on those conditions that make people less than God intended them to be.
- Preaching is not condemning those whose culture and ways of doing things are different from our own.

- Preaching is the recognition that God is the God of all people everywhere.
- Preaching is not the upbuilding of one group of people at the expense or to the detriment of another group.

- Preaching is the proclamation of God's love. *forgiveness*
- Preaching is not the instigation of violence, revenge, or hatred of any kind.

- Preaching is the truth of the gospel of Jesus Christ, made relevant for the situation in which hearers find themselves.
- Preaching is not an opportunity for the preacher to expound pet theories or ideas or to dwell entirely either in the past or in the future.

- Preaching is a joy-filled experience that lifts both hearers and preacher, not by the talent of the preacher but by the presence of God, who speaks through the preacher in spite of her or himself.
- Preaching is not a chore, an assignment, or a duty to be carried out grudgingly.
- Preaching is the humble communication in awed respect of the message God is seeking to have proclaimed through human agents.
- Preaching is not the demonstration of the preacher's intelligence, scholarship, cleverness, or winsome ways with words.
- Preaching is first and always the proclamation of God's word.
- Preaching is not the proclamation of our word but the proclamation of God's word.

And to go preach is what God has called you to do.

Not So Sure?

If you've read this far, you may have a slight uncomfortable feeling. That feeling can best be summarized in a simple question: Did God really call me to preach, or am I just imagining this?

First, let me assure you that every person who ever felt the call to preach had those same doubts. The Gospels don't tell us everything about the first apostles, but we can imagine that at times Peter and Andrew, and James and John, may have had some slight second thoughts about leaving everything they knew and following this wandering rabbi.

Second, let me assure you that every person who ever preached felt a wave of cold chills the first time she or he approached the pulpit. In the moments before the sermon began, she or he had a sudden thought, *What am I doing here?* Most preachers offer a prayer just before they preach, and many of them add a moment of silent prayer to that pre-sermon prayer time. Yes, they are certainly seeking God's will and God's words, but in a deeply human sense they are also taking a moment for their hearts to stop pounding and to get a good deep breath before they begin. I'd almost go so far as to say that a preacher who doesn't experience this near panic just as the sermon begins is not taking this God-given task with enough seriousness.

Third, let's rely on the Scriptures again. Read Acts, chapter 5. Yes, this chapter contains many important ideas, but look closely at Gamaliel's comments in verses 38b and 39. (That *b* means the second half of the verse; obviously, an *a* points to the first half of a verse.) Gamaliel's point was simply this: If what these men are doing is their own doing, it will fail. But if it is from God, it will succeed and nothing we can do will stop it.

It's the same way with your call to preach. You'll know if it is from God or is simply a momentary whim of yours by the way it proceeds. Let me give you an example from my own life: When I finally decided to pursue what I thought was God's call to preach, I was amazed by how God opened doors and enabled the process to unfold. I was in the Army, and my undergraduate degree had nothing whatsoever to do with preparation for ministry. But the only seminary to which I applied accepted me despite my background and my poor college grades. Money was a big problem, but I was astounded when several unexpected scholarships came through that enabled me to go to seminary. Where were we going to live in a strange city a couple thousand miles from home? At the last moment, an apartment became available in a married-students dormitory. I'm still convinced that these things were more than coincidence; my sense of God's call to enter the ministry was being validated.

Get the idea? The fact that you're reading this book and preparing to participate in the Lay Speaking Ministries Advanced Course on preaching may be validating your call to preach. Trust that call. Trust God. Trust yourself. You've come this far, so believe in your call.

Most of the rest of this book will be just what its title says: a primer, hints on planning, preparing, and delivering a sermon. It's a beginning book on preaching, a place to begin (not to end). Read it, discuss it, disagree with it, use it, apply it.

Go preach!

2

IT'S NOT THE CENTER

The Role of the Sermon in the Service of Worship

What Time Is Preaching?

One Saturday afternoon, shortly after I had moved to Tennessee and was pastoring an open-country small-membership congregation, the telephone rang at home and a voice with an unmistakably rural Tennessee accent on the other end greeted me. The woman asked if I was the preacher at such and such church. When I told her that I was, she asked, "What time is preaching there on Sunday?"

Our service of worship started at eleven, so I figured that I usually began preaching about eleven twenty-five or so. Is that what this caller wanted to know? I wasn't sure. I stumbled around for a moment, made some more small talk, then finally realized that she was referring to the entire Sunday morning service of worship as "preaching."

When I checked that out with some friends, they told me that it was quite common in many parts of the country to call the worship service preaching. My caller simply wanted to know what time the service of worship took place at that rural congregation.

This whole episode set my teeth on edge (to use a biblical metaphor). And in the many years I pastored that and several other rural congregations, time and again I heard the Sunday morning service of worship called the preaching. While I know that for some people preaching is the reason they attend church on Sunday, I still have the same negative reaction to considering preaching more important than other elements of the service of worship.

- The sermon, preaching, is not the focal point of the service of worship.
- The sermon is not the highlight or the center of the worship service.
- We do not gather as a congregation every Sunday morning just to listen to preaching.
- The entire service of worship does not revolve around the pastor's sermon.
- The sermon is not the most important thing that happens when the congregation gathers on Sunday morning.

Get the point. As important as preaching (the sermon) is, the sermon is not the highlight of Sunday morning for Christians. And any preacher who starts believing that what he or she has to say from behind the pulpit is what Sunday morning worship is all about is in for some major difficulties as long as that perception lasts.

If Not the Sermon, Then What?

Enough negative examples; you've got the point. So, let's try some positive statements:

- The reason Christians gather on Sunday morning is to worship God.
- The focal point of any service of worship is the people's worship of God.
- The people's praise and worship, their prayers and petitions, are the highlight of any service of worship.
- People worship when they participate in the service of worship, when they participate intellectually, emotionally, and physically (as when they are singing, reciting the creed or the prayers, or reading the Scriptures).

Put another way, people are not worshiping God as they sit passively in the pews listening to someone talk at them. Listening to a sermon is seldom a worshipful experience. It may be an educational experience; it may be an inspirational experience; it may be a challenging experience. But it is not (or is seldom) an experience of worship.

People are not worshiping God when they are doing nothing, and many people are doing nothing as they listen to the pastor's sermon. (Maybe I should modify that a bit: I've known people who made out grocery lists, balanced their checkbooks, thumbed through the hymnal, and simply daydreamed through the sermon. These people are doing something, but it is not worship.)

You're asking a good question: "How did the preaching of the sermon come to have such a central place in worship?" We can look at church history to answer that.

While preaching has always been a part of the communication of the gospel, it was not until the Protestant Reformation of the sixteenth century that preaching really came to the fore.

Worship in the Roman Catholic Church, of which almost everyone in Europe was a part before the Reformation, focused on the Eucharist (or the Holy Communion). The highlight of worship was the moment when the priest lifted the bread and prayed, and the bread was transformed into the body of Christ (by what we know as transubstantiation, but that's another book).

When Martin Luther and others broke away from Roman Catholicism over a number of issues, they actively rejected much of the Roman Catholic worship they had known. Many of the newly created groups no longer celebrated Holy Communion every Sunday. At the same time, these break-away groups insisted that worship (and the Bible) be in the language of the people, not in an obscure intellectual language such as Latin. So, the focus of worship subtly shifted from participating in the drama of the Eucharist to participating as a learner as the Scripture was read in a language all could understand and interpreted by one who was trained in such interpretation. Thus, preaching became central and remained so for many years.

The pendulum has slowly but surely swung back, however, so that our worship is a balance of participation in the drama of worship and an experience of edification through the sermon.

Where Does the Sermon Fit?

That is exactly the right question, and the last word of the question is crucial. The sermon must *fit* with the rest of the elements of the worship service—that is, the service must be an integrated whole, with all the parts of the service fitting together into a coherent whole.

At one time, worship services offered many unconnected parts and pieces, little bits here and there that had no relationship one to another. The thinking at that time was that if the service offered enough different pieces, each worshiper would find something that spoke to her or him. Fortunately, this scattershot approach quickly died out, and integrated, unified services of worship again took their place as the norm. But elements of that scattershot approach persist in the call that some lay speakers get: "You just come and preach about anything you want to preach about. Our lay leader will take care of the rest of the service." (Don't agree to that kind of invitation. But more about that later.)

The sermon has to fit in; it has to be part of an integrated or unified whole. Fit into what? Be part of an integrated what? The sermon has to fit into and be part of an integrated, unified service of worship. What does that mean? It means a service of worship that includes the traditional components or elements of worship, the components or elements that make up and complete an experience of worship for the congregation as a community and for the individual members of that congregation. And what are those components or elements of worship that have to work together to provide this overall experience? You'll find them on pages two and three through five in *The United Methodist Hymnal*. (You do have a copy of *The United Methodist Hymnal*, don't you?)

Wait. I know there's a turnoff word in that previous paragraph. That word is *traditional*. You might prefer contemporary worship, praise worship, or informal worship—or whatever name you might call it—and you might see your style of worship as the opposite of traditional worship. But the fact is, even the most contemporary worship uses the same elements or components of worship that the so-called traditional style uses. These components and forms are long-standing and are part of our Christian heritage. Whether your worship is traditional or contemporary, the forms are the same; the expressions might be different. In other words, the elements of worship have come down to us across the centuries from ancient synagogues and early churches and have remained unchanged in form (but often changed in expression) over two thousand years.

But if your service of worship—be it traditional or contemporary or anything else—is lacking these basic elements, then the congregation is experiencing worship that is less than complete and is being entertained instead of led.

We'll now look at the crucial components of worship. Along the way, we'll make some comments about being sure that the service is an integrated, whole experience.

Let's go back to page 3 in *The United Methodist Hymnal.*

The Entrance

A service of worship begins with the Entrance, the coming together of God's people for praise and worship. People come together in a variety of ways. In some congregations, people have not seen one another since last Sunday and need to do some catching up. If the church has a narthex (a hallway or vestibule outside the sanctuary), this is the place for such fellowship to take place. Then, as people enter the sanctuary and find their seats, they can adopt a more reverent mood and listen, pray, and meditate as music is played.

But if the church building does not have a narthex or other area suitable for this fellowship, such fellowship is perfectly appropriate within the sanctuary prior to the time of worship. Usually, the pastor, lay leader, liturgist, or someone else ends this fellowship time with a word of welcome and thanksgiving for everyone's presence. (Please never say something such as, "Well, it's about time to get started." Talk about setting teeth on edge!)

You'll see in the materials under the Entrance in the *Hymnal* that this gathering time is where announcements belong. Announcements, meeting reminders, upcoming events, birthdays and anniversaries, and other congregational news are crucial to the fellowship life of the congregation. But they do not belong in the middle of the worship service, for they can be intrusive there. They belong here at the beginning, as the people gather and prepare for worship.

Following the announcements, the mood shifts slightly toward a greater acknowledgement of God's presence as a Greeting, Call to Worship, or other Scripture sentences are used. What's a Call to Worship or a Greeting? Get familiar with *The United Methodist Book of Worship*, where you'll find appropriate Greetings and Scripture sentences at the beginning of each section of "The Christian Year." (But you'll read more about that in Chapter 4.)

Part of this Entrance is a hymn, either before or after the Greeting. This hymn should be a hymn of praise and thanksgiving, a hymn ascribing God majesty and glory, a hymn of joy and wonder in the presence of God. Hymns such as "O For a Thousand Tongues to Sing" or "Holy, Holy, Holy" are appropriate here. "Rock of Ages" or "Just As I Am," although great hymns, do not belong here.

A prayer usually follows these elements of Entrance. That prayer is often called an Invocation; that is, a prayer asking or invoking God's presence in the time of worship. Again, you'll find prayers of invocation by seasons in "The Christian Year" in *The Book of Worship.*

While this is not listed on page 3 in the *Hymnal,* many congregations include in the Entrance the congregational recitation of an affirmation of faith. In this sense, the worshipers are acknowledging and claiming what they believe. See 880 through 889 in the *Hymnal* for appropriate affirmations of faith or creeds. This affirmation is usually followed by the "Gloria Patri" (*Hymnal,* 70 and 71).

Are you getting a sense of the flow here? The members of the congregation assemble, share in fellowship, praise God, seek God's presence throughout the time of worship, affirm their belief in God, then praise God once again.

Proclamation and Response

Are you still on page 3 in *The United Methodist Hymnal?* If so, you'll see that the Proclamation and Response follows the Entrance. And what is the Proclamation and Response? Look at page 4 in the *Hymnal.* The Proclamation and Response time is for the Scripture readings and for the message of the service, the sermon, or other means of proclaiming the word of God. The Scripture or the sermon might be preceded by a choir anthem or by special music, but this music must be selected with an eye toward the overall integration of the service of worship. Frequently, this time preceding the sermon is when a children's time is observed, often with a Scripture reading and then an informal sharing time with the children in which the Scripture is discussed and perhaps enacted or memorized.

The important dimension of the United Methodist order of worship is that the Scripture lessons and the sermon come early in the service of worship. Yes, I know that in many rural congregations the sermon is one of the final components of the service of worship, followed only by a hymn and the benediction. Putting the sermon late in the service allows the congregation no time to respond to the Scripture and the sermon. And it is the response of the congregation to the word of God, read from the Scripture and interpreted through the sermon (or other means), that is the heart or focus of the service of worship.

Notice the responses to the Word on page 4 in the *Hymnal.* Suitable responses might be an invitation to discipleship or a commitment to the congregation. It might be the recitation of a creed or affirmation of faith, if this has not been used earlier in the service. It might be any of the rituals of the church, such as baptism, confirmation, or even baptismal reaffirmation. Often, the response to the Word begins with an appropriate hymn, one keyed to the Word that has been proclaimed.

This note of congregational response, actual participation in the service, continues as the members of the gathered community lift up prayers of praise and concerns. The prayer might be a bidding prayer (the liturgist invites the congregation to pray aloud or in silence their thanksgivings, intercessions, petitions, confessions, and commitments). Or it could take the form of a pastoral prayer or a prayer offered by a member of the congregation. Frequently, this prayer leads into the whole congregation united in our Lord's Prayer.

The congregational response continues as the members of the gathered community participate in the offering. They are given an opportunity to present God's tithes and their own gifts and offerings. While these offerings are often in a monetary form, they need not be restricted to this. Gifts might include canned goods for a food pantry, written commitments to participate in the ministries of the congregation, and on and on. We narrow our people's understanding of offering gifts to God when we limit those gifts to money. Note that the offering is presenting to

God God's tithes and our offerings and gifts. The tithe, the tenth, already belongs to God. It is not our offering or our gift, for it is God's already. Gifts and offerings include that which we give over and above the tithe.

The Thanksgiving

If the Sacrament of the Lord's Supper is to be observed, it becomes the focal point of the Thanksgiving. If Communion is not scheduled, then the Thanksgiving can take the form of a prayer, an anthem or special music, and our Lord's Prayer, if it was not used during the Proclamation and Response.

Sending Forth

The final component of worship is the Sending Forth. A congregational hymn of commitment and challenge is used at this time to inspire members of the congregation to live out their discipleship each day. This hymn is followed by a Dismissal With Blessing or a Benediction (both mean somewhat the same thing).

That's the way worship is conducted within United Methodist congregations. Through this format, we can put the emphasis of worship where it belongs: on the praise of God, the proclamation of the Word, and the response of the people.

Get It Together

These, then, are the elements or components of any service of worship, be that worship in what we call the traditional mode or in the contemporary mode. The music may differ, the preaching styles may differ, the way the congregations respond may differ, but every service of worship includes the Entrance, the Proclamation and Response, the Thanksgiving, and the Sending Forth.

Naming these elements in your Sunday worship bulletin is most appropriate, for it helps your congregation understand the flow of the service of worship. You might even modify these titles a bit. For example, the bulletin used in the congregation I serve lists these elements: We Gather as the People of God, We Hear and Respond to God's Word, We Give Thanks and Praise to God, and We Go Into the World as Disciples.

But—and this is critical—these elements must work together to provide worshipers with an integrated, unified experience of worship. These four components, and the pieces that make up each element, must all work together, work in concert, so that people experience the worship service as a whole. Hymns, special music, prayers, Scripture, sermon—all of these must revolve around a central theme or common core of the worship service. (Where does that theme come from? Good question. The best answer is the lectionary. We'll get into that in detail in Chapter 4.)

Few things are more disruptive of a true worship experience than a component or a piece of a component that just doesn't fit with the others. Imagine what effect on the joyous Easter celebration a sad and mournful anthem might have. Or if the entire service of worship is focusing on our need to repent of our sins, reading Psalm 150 responsively might not be the wisest choice of Scripture. Notice that this is not a critique of Psalm 150 or of a sad and mournful anthem; these have their place. But whatever pieces of an element or component are used must all fit, mesh, work together to provide the congregation with a true experience of worship.

And the sermon, that message you've worked so long and hard to prepare, is just one of those pieces. It's not the whole show.

3
GOOD NEWS

The Sermon as a Proclamation of the Good News

> Go therefore and make disciples of all nations, baptizing them
> in the name of the Father and of the Son and of the Holy
> Spirit, and teaching them to obey everything that I have com-
> manded you. And remember, I am with you always, to the end
> of the age. (Matthew 28:19-20)

The Great Commission is our charter for preaching, for proclaiming the good news of the gospel of Jesus Christ. We preach because Christ called us to preach. We preach because Christ commanded us to preach. We preach because we are disciples, servants, of the Lord Jesus Christ. We preach because we cannot keep from preaching. Praise be to God!

But what do we preach? What do we say? What is our message? Answers to those questions are fairly easy to state.

- We preach the good news of the gospel.
- We lift up the Lord Jesus Christ.

Our preaching must be a telling and retelling of the story of all that God has done and is doing for God's people. Our preaching must be a telling and retelling of the love, grace, and forgiveness extended to us by an infinitely loving God. Our preaching must be a telling and retelling of Emmanuel (God is with us, no matter what).

And our preaching must glorify the Lord Jesus Christ in and through all that we say and the way we say it. Jesus Christ is the word of God made flesh; Jesus Christ is God come to live our lives with us; Jesus Christ is God incarnate. That is why our preaching must glorify and lift up Christ.

All of this means that our preaching is God- and Christ-centered, not human-centered. We proclaim what God through Christ has done, is doing, and will do. We announce Christ as the answer, the solution, the remedy. We proclaim Christ as the Way, the Truth, and the Light. We, of course, do this by talking about our human condition and the situations in which we find ourselves. But our preaching is not about us; it is about God: God in Christ and the Holy Spirit.

This may seem obvious. But if it is, then why are our sermons about us? Why are we so tempted to spend our time talking about what we think, what we do, what we want, or the errors we see in others? Many sermons spend twenty minutes cataloging the ills of society or the shortcomings of a particular situation, but they have less than a minute left to proclaim the good news of Christ.

Again, why is this so?

- Is it because it's easier for us to talk about things we know than about things we don't know? Do we know (or at least think we know) what's going on in our world, but deep down we don't know the good news of God's word?
- Or is it because we like to talk about what we think of God and the things of faith rather than what God's word tells us about God and the things of faith?
- Or is it because we have just read a book and want to relate everything we discovered in that book? An old cliché that is unfortunately quite true is, "I believe the last book I read."

I recall a friend who often announced that he had just read a book that was going to change his life completely. We chuckled that if he changed his life by every book he read, he'd be on a permanent pinwheel. Understand that this is not an indictment of reading books—preachers are called to be avid readers and students—but it is an indictment of the temptation all preachers face to summarize the last books they read in their next sermons.

So, What Is the Problem?

Let's put it bluntly: We are called to proclaim the word of God, the Scriptures, but we don't know the Scriptures well. The Bible is the basic, fundamental, absolutely essential text for preaching. And the reality is that we don't know the Bible as we should; we don't read the Bible as we should; we don't study the Bible as we should. As a result, our preaching is often a classic example of proof-texting or some interpretation that may or may not be consistent with the message of the Scripture.

What is proof-texting? That's what we do when we find a Scripture verse we think supports our position and then use it to make our argument, even though we may be using the Scripture text inappropriately.

A quick and obvious example is people quoting Matthew 7:1 ("Do not judge, so that you may not be judged") as a reason for not helping a friend or relative straighten out her or his life. But that verse needs to be read in conjunction with verse 2 ("For with the judgment you make you will be judged"). This casts the verse in a different light, for it says that we are to judge one another so long as we are willing to be judged by the same criteria we use to judge another. We need to read and apply Matthew 7:1 in conjunction with other verses, such as Matthew 18:15; Galatians 6:1; and James 5:19-20, to cite a few of many examples.

Proof-texting has been used to justify prejudice and racism, slavery and gross economic advantage, child abuse and a second-class status for women, war and persecutions, and a multitude of other things that are clearly not part of the gospel.

And proof-texting continues as one of the great temptations facing preachers, especially those who are beginning their preaching ministries or who have little experience in preaching.

How Can We Know the Scriptures?

I would guess that the statement about not knowing the Scriptures as well as we should would apply to just about everyone. I can't imagine anyone saying that he or she knows the Scriptures so well that there is no longer any need to study. The question becomes, "How can we immerse ourselves in regular Scripture study in order to equip us to proclaim God's word (not ours) and to proclaim it with truth and honesty?"

Here are some hints:

1. *Regularly read and study the Bible.* Ideally, find two times each day that you can devote to living in God's word of the Scriptures. Make one of these times a time of study, of concentrated digging into the Scriptures, of searching for understanding and insight into the words that you read, of comprehending what the original writer was saying and to whom that writer was saying these words. This is study time.

   The second time you spend with the Scriptures each day ought to be a meditative and devotional time. Let the Scriptures speak to you and address your own life situation. Read the Scriptures prayerfully, seeking God's particular word for you in that Scripture.

I recall attending a New Testament Bible study class in a seminary one summer. We dug deep into the background of the Gospels, studied some of the original languages, and learned much about Judea of the first century. Then, on one of the days of the class, we all arrived at eight in the morning, pencils poised for another day of extensive note taking. But the professor surprised us by giving each of us a small slip of paper with one verse of a Gospel written on it. He said, "Go outside, wander around the grounds of the school, and concentrate on the verse in your hand. Let it seep into you. Let it speak to you. Do this until four this afternoon; then come back and tell us what you've found." I thought it was a silly assignment; I wanted to do depth study on the context of the Gospels. I reluctantly read my verse, went outside, and tried to think about it. I wandered the paths around the seminary for a few hours trying to think about that verse. And slowly but surely, the meaning of that verse—for me, not for some scholar somewhere—started to seep into my consciousness. I heard Jesus speaking to me and my life through that verse. I began to experience that verse and to see what directions in life that verse of Scripture was calling me to take.

That's the word of God when we dwell on it and let it into our lives. The New International Version of the Bible says that all Scripture is breathed on by God (2 Timothy 3:16). As God breathed on that handful of dirt in Genesis 2:7 and it became a living human being, and as God breathed on those dry bones in Ezekiel, chapter 37, and the bones became alive, so can and will God make the Scriptures come alive in us when we spend enough time to let them seep into us and speak to our deepest lives.

2. *Get involved in some form of group Bible study and keep at it.* Sunday school is excellent, but get in a Bible study group beyond Sunday school. When you select a Bible study group, be sure that the materials used in the study lead the group toward studying the Bible itself, not what someone has written about the Bible or an interpretation of the Bible. Now, this does not mean to read a verse and to tell what it means. That is often a pooling of ignorance. Watch out for so-called Bible studies that are thinly veiled arguments for particular positions or opinions using the Bible as a proof-text for someone's hobbyhorse. An example of this are the Bible studies that emerged just before the turn of the millennium. Many of them were caught up in the Y2K hysteria and were so-called proofs that the end of time was upon us as the calendar turned.

One of the best of many good group Bible studies available is DISCIPLE, a comprehensive, in-depth study of the Scriptures that requires a major commitment on the part of participants. Available as a survey ("Becoming Disciples Through Bible Study"), as a study of Genesis through Exodus and Luke through Acts ("Into the Word, Into the World"), as a study of the prophets and the epistles of Paul ("Remember Who You Are"), and as a study of the Old Testament writings and the Johanine materials in the New Testament ("Under the Tree of Life"), DISCIPLE is a thirty-four week study that requires participation in weekly two-and-a-half-hour group sessions as well as about an hour of Bible reading and study each day.

Other solid Bible studies are the Kerygma materials, *Seasons of the Spirit* (devoted to lectionary Bible study), *The Grand Sweep: 365 Days From Genesis Through Revelation* (the study of the entire Bible in one year), the "Genesis to Revelation" series, and the "Journey Through the Bible" series, to name just a few.

Join a lectionary Bible study group in your community. (You'll read more about the lectionary in the next chapter.) A lectionary Bible study group often has preaching as a focus, so such a group will help you begin to learn how to form sermons from the texts of the Bible. No, you don't have to be preaching on a regular basis to be part of a lectionary Bible study group. And, yes, be prepared for some new and different ideas because most lectionary Bible study groups are ecumenical; that is, people from various denominations gather together to study the Scriptures. Ask your pastor about lectionary Bible study groups in your area.

3. *Develop your own Bible study library*—and use it. What should a solid Bible study library include as a beginning? Here's a brief, illustrative list:

- At least three different translations (not paraphrases) of the Bible. For a start, get the New Revised Standard Version, the New International Version, the Contemporary English Version or the Today's English Version, and perhaps the King James Version. Get study Bibles, if possible. But always keep in mind that the notes in study Bibles are not part of the Scriptures. These notes are the editor's or the commentator's ideas about the Scriptures.

- At least two Bible dictionaries. Why two? Because even dictionaries are written with particular interpretative and theological slants. You'll gain more than twice as much insight by consulting at least two Bible dictionaries.

- A solid Bible atlas. We often forget that the Bible took place in time and space. A freestanding atlas (not just the handful of maps in the back of your study Bible) is indispensable for serious and careful Bible study. But don't just have an atlas; learn how to use it. The geography of Palestine has often been called the Fifth Gospel, for the land shaped much of the history of Israel and of the New Testament.

- At least two (preferably three) Bible commentaries. A commentary is just what the title suggests: a list of comments about the Scriptures, usually prepared by a scholar or groups of scholars. A preacher must have at a minimum two commentaries. Otherwise, the preacher may begin to believe that the perspective in the one commentary is the only perspective or the right perspective. Tragically, I've heard many sermons that were nothing but a rehash of what a commentary writer had to say about a text, with no attempt made to see that text from a different vantage point. As crucial to comprehending the Bible as commentaries are, they are not the Scripture itself. Commentaries help illuminate the Bible, but they are not the Bible, even if you find yourself agreeing consistently with the interpretations of a single commentary.

- As complete a concordance as you can afford. A concordance is a basic Bible study tool, for it lists the words in the Bible in alphabetical order and then cites every passage in the Bible in which that word appears. Some concordances are described as exhaustive, which means that they list every word in the Bible and every place every word appears. Other concordances are less than exhaustive, listing only major words. Many study Bibles have a concordance in the study aids section, usually in the back. But in most cases, these concordances are too limited to be of much use. A preacher is better off purchasing an exhaustive concordance for the particular version of the Bible she or he is using.

  Here's a quick example: Suppose you wanted to find the passage "No testing has overtaken you that is not common to everyone." You remember this verse from somewhere, but you're not even sure if you're remembering it accurately. Which word might you use to find this text? Words such as *no, has, you, that, is, not, to,* and even *everyone* are too vague and general. Try the word *testing.* You'll find every verse in which this word appears and discover that your verse comes from 1 Corinthians 10:13. But you will also want to track down some of the other uses of the word *testing,* as listed in the concordance, in order to get a better idea of what the Bible means when it uses this word.

See "A Beginning Preacher's Library" (pages 125–26) for an illustrative list of these Bible study tools.

Mark It Up

When I was a child, I was taught to never put anything on top of a Bible, to never open a Bible unless I had washed my hands first, to never drop a Bible, and to never, never make any kind of mark in the Bible (except for the presentation page, where it was written that I had been given my first Bible for a year's perfect attendance in Sunday school).

In fact, not until I entered seminary and bought a study Bible did I have the nerve to make notes and mark passages in my Bible. In seminary I learned what I should have known all along: The Bible is a living book, and you and I are to have dialog with it. One of the best ways to dialog with it is to underline, highlight, and make marginal notes; in short, to use it.

I recall in my first student appointment visiting two families one summer afternoon. The first family proudly showed me the family Bible, which was resting comfortably in a place of honor on the coffee table. That Bible, I was told, had been in the family for three generations. As I picked it up and thumbed through it, I noticed that many of the pages were still stuck together, the way pages in a new, unused, gilt-edged book often stick together until they are turned. I thought something was wrong.

Then I visited the second home. When I arrived, the young mother was sitting at her kitchen table reading her Bible while waiting for the load of clothes to dry. She quickly shut the Bible and put it on one of the kitchen chairs as I walked in. I asked if I could see the Bible. It was a recent edition of the Bible, but all the pages were dog-eared, with notes in the margins in several different colors of ink and pencil. I could identify coffee stains and even cookie crumbs on some of the pages. I asked about what looked like dried-up wet spots on some pages, and the young mother sheepishly told me that those were tear stains. That Bible was one of the most beautiful Bibles I have ever seen because it was a living Bible, living with her and her family, a daily companion on the walk of life. That's what a Bible is.

You have been called to proclaim the good news of Jesus Christ. Immerse yourself in God's Word so that the Word may come alive in you.

4

THE LECTIONARY OR NOT?

The Values of Lectionary Preaching

So, you've been called to preach; you have a grasp of what preaching is and what it isn't; and you want to proclaim the good news of the gospel of Jesus Christ in every one of your sermons.

Great. You're right on target. But about what are you going to preach?

Let's put that another way: If you're filling the pulpit of a church, perhaps as an interim or perhaps because you've been appointed by the district superintendent to serve a charge, you have to come up with a sermon every 168 hours. That's right. Every week, at least once a week, people are expecting you to proclaim God's word in an inspiring and challenging way.

So, what's going to be the subject of your sermon next Sunday? And how do you decide what the subject will be? Where do you get the ideas around which to develop your sermon?

If you are anything like I was when I first started preaching many years ago, you already have several great sermon ideas. I know I had about half a dozen sermons burning inside me that I wanted to preach, and I couldn't wait for a chance to get up and preach them.

But I quickly discovered that only several of those great and earth-changing ideas could be developed into a full sermon, and that a couple of those ideas were tied to certain events and seasons so that those messages would not be appropriate at all times and all places. So, in that first congregation I served while still a seminary student, the congregation heard during my first two Sundays what I thought were my two dynamite sermons. But then I was hit with a cold chill the next Monday morning because I had no great ideas for the coming Sunday. I had fewer than 150 hours to come up with something to preach that would at least match those first two sermons. I also had to go to classes and study for my seminary courses. Where in the world was I going to get a great sermon idea for the coming Sunday?

You and I have a great answer to that question: We preach the lectionary.

What Is the Lectionary?

OK, we preach the lectionary. But what in the world is that? A lectionary is a system of Bible readings for every Sunday and holy day throughout the liturgical year. The lectionary we use (*The Revised Common Lectionary*) consists of three Scripture readings for each Sunday: an Old Testament reading, a reading from the Epistles, and a reading from the Gospels. In addition, the lectionary suggests a psalm to be used as a response and mediation. These readings (each reading for a given Sunday is called a lection) were chosen to emphasize the liturgical year, and together they will provide a solid experience of worship and praise built around them.

The Liturgical Year

But before we get into the lectionary further, let's take a quick sidetrack around another term that may not be as familiar to you as you might wish. That term is *liturgical year.*

The liturgical year is a year-long observance of the life and ministry of Jesus Christ and the church begun in his name. It includes all the great festivals of the Christian faith and helps us relive, year after year, the story of the Gospels and the early church.

The liturgical year covers twelve months, but they are not the twelve calendar months. Instead, each liturgical year begins with Advent, the four Sundays of preparation for the birth of Jesus Christ. Often, these are the four Sundays in December preceding Christmas, although on many years the last Sunday in November is the first Sunday in Advent.

Next comes the Christmas season, a two-week celebration of Jesus' birth. It starts with Christmas Eve and Christmas Day and ends on January 6, the great celebration of Epiphany, which commemorates the revelation of the Christ to the Gentiles through the metaphor of the coming of the wise men (Matthew 2:1-12).

The season after the Epiphany begins with a Sunday recalling the baptism of Jesus Christ by John the Baptist and ends with the last Sunday before Ash Wednesday. This last Sunday is the celebration of the transfiguration of Jesus Christ on the mountaintop with his closest disciples (Matthew 17:1-8; Mark 9:2-8; Luke 9:28-36).

The penitential season of Lent, a time of preparing our souls for the great Easter celebration, begins with Ash Wednesday and continues for forty days (not counting the Sundays during the season). Lent includes six Sundays. The sixth Sunday observes both Jesus' entry into Jerusalem (Palm Sunday) and the Passion of Jesus. Lent continues through Holy Week with Holy Thursday (often called Maundy Thursday; the word *maundy* means command); Good Friday, the day of the Crucifixion; and Holy Saturday.

Christ is risen. He is risen indeed! Lent leads toward a glorious celebration on Easter Day of the resurrection of Jesus Christ, the first day of the Easter season. Following Easter Day, the church remembers Christ walking among his disciples after the Resurrection. The Easter season includes the celebration of the ascension of Jesus Christ and ends with the exciting day of Pentecost, when the apostles received the Holy Spirit and added greatly to their number (Acts 2).

The first Sunday after Pentecost Sunday is observed as Trinity Sunday, when we remember God in Three Persons. Then follow a number of Sundays in what is known as the season after Pentecost (sometimes called Ordinary Time or Kingdom-tide). When this season is called Ordinary Time, the word *ordinary* does not mean boring or everyday. Rather, it means that during this time we do not celebrate any specific part of the life of Jesus or the early church. During Ordinary Time, worship emphasizes the constant and recurring components of the service of worship, such as the creed, the doxology and Gloria Patri, the Lord's Prayer, and so forth.

The season after Pentecost includes Reformation Sunday, commemorating the Protestant Reformation of the sixteenth century; All Saints' Sunday; and, for those of us in the United States of America, Thanksgiving. The season after Pentecost culminates in the last Sunday after Pentecost, known as Christ the King Sunday.

The next Sunday is the first Sunday in Advent, which begins the cycle of the liturgical year again.

Thus, being aware of the Christian Year helps us and helps our people learn and understand the story of Christ Jesus our Lord and of the early church. Changing the colors of the vestments (the cloths covering the Communion table and the pulpit and the stoles clergy wear) reminds congregations of the Christian Year and of the story of Jesus the Christ.

What does this say for preaching? Among other things, it suggests that we would probably not preach a Christmas sermon during the season of Lent (when we are preparing for Easter) or would not offer a sermon that details the crucifixion of Jesus during the season after Pentecost.

An awareness of the Christian Year keeps us focused.

Back to the Lectionary

So, the lectionary is a list of biblical readings for each Sunday and Holy Day in the Christian Year, beginning with the first Sunday in Advent and ending with the last Sunday after Pentecost, Christ the King Sunday. Each Sunday's and each Holy Day's list of reading consists of three lections—a reading from the Old Testament, a reading from the Epistles, and a reading from the Gospels—all carefully chosen to support a common theme or emphasis for preaching and worshiping. And a psalm is suggested for response and meditation in worship.

But lest we think the lectionary is something new, remember that the lectionary is at least as old as the first century. Synagogues of the first century had fixed Scripture readings for the sabbath and for feast days. Remember Jesus in Luke, chapter 4? When Jesus was given the scroll of the prophet Isaiah, he turned to the reading for the day, read that passage, and then told those in the synagogue that that prophecy had been fulfilled in him (Luke 4:14-30).

Throughout the history of Christianity, lectionaries of various types have been used to guide public worship and preaching. Some of these lectionaries contained only three lections for each Sunday, others as many as five. Martin Luther used the lectionary of his day, and John Wesley preached from the lectionary used by the Church of England in his day.

For a time in some Protestant churches, lectionary preaching fell out of favor, as preachers preferred to select their own texts or to preach topical sermons. But slowly the widespread use of the lectionary has come back into many Protestant (as well as Roman Catholic and Eastern Orthodox) worship services.

The lectionary used by The United Methodist Church is *The Revised Common Lectionary* of 1992. This is called a *common* lectionary because it is used in common by many major Protestant denominations. And it is called the *revised* lectionary because it has been subject to revision from time to time by a group of scholars representing the several Protestant denominations who share in the use of this lectionary.

The Revised Common Lectionary covers three years, called simply Year A, Year B, and Year C. Each year begins with the first Sunday in Advent and continues through the end of the season after Pentecost (or the last Sunday after Pentecost).

Therefore, to know what the lections for a given Sunday are, you would need to know if this particular year is A, B, or C and what Sunday within the liturgical year a particular Sunday is.

Then where would you find the lections or the readings for that Sunday? You would look in *The United Methodist Book of Worship*, starting on page 227. (You do have a copy of *The Book of Worship*, don't you?) Notice that you can find the lections for any Sunday from 1992 through 2020 on this chart. Locate the liturgical year in which you now are (remember, starting with Advent); then locate on the following pages the readings for that particular Sunday.

For example, I am writing this in mid-November 2001. Thus, we are in Year C, because this liturgical year began with Advent of the year 2000. This coming Sunday is November 18, so I can find the readings for the "Sunday between November 13 and 19 inclusive" on page 237 in *The Book of Worship*. Note that the lections are Isaiah 65:17-25; 2 Thessalonians 3:6-13; and Luke 21:5-19. For the response meditation, there is a choice between Isaiah 12 and Psalm 118 (responsive reading 839 in *The United Methodist Hymnal*).

I have my three lections or lessons and a psalm or other reading for a response. I will build a service of worship and a sermon using these passages. That's using the lectionary.

Here are some other places you can find the lections for any given Sunday. (All are available from Cokesbury, 800-672-1789.)
- *The Abingdon Worship Planning Calendar*
- *The United Methodist Calendar and Workbook*
- *The United Methodist Program Calendar*
- *Prepare!: A Weekly Worship Planbook for Pastors and Musicians*
- *The New Handbook of the Christian Year*

The last two list appropriate hymns tied to the lections for each Sunday in the year. The *Handbook* suggests calls to worship, invocations, and collects (short prayers).

You can also find ecumenical church calendars that list lectionary readings. The Abingdon *Word Alive* Sunday bulletin service lists the lections for each week on page 4 of the bulletin cover.

Preaching the Lectionary

While the lections have been chosen because they relate one to another (and occasionally to the Sunday lections the week before and the week following), preaching the lectionary does not necessarily mean using all the Scripture passages directly in the sermon. But it does mean using the lections within the whole, integrated service of praise and worship:

- You may choose to use the reading from the Psalms as a congregational responsive reading. Many of the psalms used as lections are arranged as responsive readings in *The United Methodist Hymnal* (pages 738–862).
- In my present appointment, I often use one of the lections as the basis for a children's meditation and then refer to this children's time as part of the sermon.
- And on some occasions, one of the lections might be fittingly sung as an anthem or as a congregational hymn. (See pages 924–26 in the *Hymnal* for a list of scriptural texts that form the basis of familiar hymns.)

In short, the lectionary readings for any given Sunday provide the basis of an integrated, unified order of worship along with the direction and the focus of the sermon that is part of that service of worship. To be genuinely worshipful, any service of worship must be planned in order to unite all the components of the service into a unified whole. This is one of the reasons a lay speaker should help plan the entire service of worship when she or he is invited to preach, rather than being told, "You just preach; we'll take care of everything else. You preach about whatever you want to talk about." Unfortunately, this latter approach is prevalent.

Why Preach the Lectionary?

You are exactly right; I've built a case for how to use the lectionary, but you may still be wondering why you should be using the lectionary (and you may be wondering if using the lectionary carries with it any drawbacks). Both of these are good questions that deserve careful answers.

1. Using the lectionary keeps our preaching focused on and in Scripture and ensures that we will cover all of Scripture through a year and certainly all of Scripture through a three-year lectionary cycle.

   We are all tempted to preach on those texts we like or those portions of Scripture that we find easy to use in sermon preparation, such as the parables or the Sermon on the Mount. But using the lectionary keeps us scripturally honest, since we have to deal with some difficult texts and with the message of the whole Bible. Seeing the relationship between an Old Testament reading and an Epistle reading may force us to stretch our minds and discover some new insights into God's word.

But we may be just as easily tempted to fall back on books of sermons based on the biblical texts in the lectionary or to rely too much on commentaries about the lections. Also, we may be tempted to take the easy way out; that is, rely on one or more of the many lectionary sermon services offered through the mail or through the Internet. When we do that, we are not preaching our sermon; we are delivering someone else's message, for we have not plumbed the depths of those texts.

2. Preaching the lectionary keeps us focused in the congregation and in the greater ecumenical church. Lectionary texts are designed to speak to congregations as well as to individuals. The gospel is for the church as well as for individual people. Lectionary preaching helps us emphasize that. This is one of the reasons the lections for each Sunday include an epistle reading. The epistles were generally written to congregations and for congregations, as well as to and for individuals.

But focusing too much on the congregational dimensions of the lectionary can make us miss the real-life needs of some members of the congregation. We are preaching to real people with real concerns. A slavish devotion to lectionary preaching could cause us to miss some of those concerns or, what is often worse, to try to wedge those concerns sideways into a scriptural text in a way that just doesn't fit.

3. Preaching the lectionary makes the Scripture primary in our preaching; that is, every sermon we preach is biblically based and grounded in Scripture. Preaching the lectionary makes us biblical preachers, and part of our task as preachers is to open the Word of God for our congregations.

But locking ourselves steadfastly into preaching the lectionary may eliminate occasional topical sermons or may interfere with what we may need to say on special and unusual occasions. Many strong lectionary preachers left the lectionary to prepare sermons for the Sunday that followed September 11, 2001. Yet, most preachers were amazed at how eloquently the lections for September and October of 2001 spoke to the crisis in which our nation found itself. Perhaps the Holy Spirit has something to do with the selection of passages for the lectionary. On occasion, though, things take place within the congregation or community that demand a topical sermon, regardless of the lectionary. I recall the slow, painful death of a young child in a congregation I served. When the little girl died on a Saturday morning, I abandoned my lectionary-based sermon and tried to preach a word of comfort to the tiny congregation that had supported the young family through the child's illness.

My conclusion? Preaching the lectionary outweighs the drawbacks that may be inherent in such preaching. I would rather trust the combined wisdom of centuries of Christian faith as well as the texts of the Scriptures than trust my own imagination to come up with a sermon idea each week. I would rather know that I am preaching the whole Bible rather than preaching just about my favorite passages. I would rather commit myself to the study and effort required for lectionary preaching than see how many different ways I can present the same topical sermon in different guises.

Any new or beginning preacher should use the lectionary. It is comprehensive; it is liturgical; it is practical; it is congregational and ecumenical; and it is soundly biblical. No preacher can do better than that.

Hint

Check in your community for a lectionary study group. In many communities, groups of pastors and laity from all denominations gather early each week to study the lectionary Scriptures for the coming Sunday and to pray for insight into those texts. Discover such a group in your community and join in, even if you are not preaching every Sunday. The group of which I am a member meets every Tuesday morning at eight-thirty to study the lections together for an hour over coffee and doughnuts. Our informal lectionary study group is a high priority on my calendar, for I am constantly amazed at the insights the others bring to the lections, insights that open familiar Scriptures to me in new and exciting ways.

5

GET READY–I

The Initial Preparation of the Sermon

Y ou've just hung up the telephone. Funny, but your mouth seems a little dry, and you have just a moment's lapse in concentration. You just said, "Yes," and now you're not absolutely sure that was a good idea. After all, you've never done this before. But you agreed to do it.

You have agreed to preach a Sunday morning sermon in front of a congregation of people you don't know. And you've never preached anywhere before. Oh, you've taught Sunday school a couple times, but that was with friends. You've also prayed in public on several occasions in your church.

But this is different. You've been asked to preach a sermon, a full sermon. You're it. Strangely enough, you've hoped this day would come, but somehow you thought you'd be better prepared for it when it came. And now you're not at all sure that you should have agreed.

Let's continue this scenario. It's Thursday evening, and the pastor from a church about twenty miles away asked if you could preach a week from this coming Sunday. The pastor, who will be out of town for a family medical situation, called the district superintendent. The district superintendent consulted her list of lay speakers, found your name and address as someone in the neighborhood, and suggested your name to the pastor. Then the pastor phoned you, and you said yes. What now?

You quickly look over the notes you made as you talked with the pastor:

1. Yes, the lay leader will serve as liturgist and will be responsible for the announcements.
2. Yes, the pastor will send you a copy of this Sunday's worship bulletin so that you can see the flow of the service.
3. Yes, the church follows the lectionary. (That will help you plan.)
4. Yes, you will be responsible only for the Scripture before the sermon, the sermon, and the benediction. A volunteer will take care of the children's time, and the president of the United Methodist Women will take care of the prayer concerns and the pastoral prayer. The lay leader will introduce you before your Scripture reading.
5. Yes, a hymn follows the sermon, and the congregation is accustomed to being invited to a silent prayer time at the chancel rail during this hymn.
6. Yes, the pastor wears a robe, but you will not be expected to do so.
7. No, the congregation has not planned any baptisms, no one is expected to present her or himself to unite with the congregation, and the sacrament of the Lord's Supper will not be observed. (If the Lord's Supper is to be observed, check again with the pastor, or with the district superintendent, right away to find out how these things can be properly handled.)
8. Yes, you can contact the person who does the worship bulletin by Tuesday afternoon of next week with your sermon title and hymn suggestions.
9. Oh, yes, the service is at ten forty-five. (That's different from your home church.) You'll want to plan to arrive at the church about ten to fifteen minutes before the service. (Should you go to Sunday school there? That's up to you. It gives you an opportunity to meet some of the people, but it also diverts your attention a little from your sermon. You be the judge on that one.)

Those nine points (in any order) make up a good checklist of things to ask when you are invited to preach. As you gain experience, you'll add other items you want to discover about where and to whom you will be preaching. But these nine constitute a good beginning point to help you know the nuts and bolts of the service and your responsibility in it.

OK. All of that is written down. You've asked all the questions you need to ask. Next step?

God Will Provide, But...

First, let's get a misconception out of the way. That misconception goes something like this:

> God called me to preach, and God will give me the words I need and
> the sermon I must deliver when I get behind the pulpit. Preparation
> and getting ready are unnecessary. All I have to do is trust God, and
> God will speak through me.

Now, some of that is true. God does provide for us and equip us to preach the Word of God, for that is the reason God called us to preach. Also, we can trust God, for God has promised to be with us—Emmanuel—no matter what we are doing and no matter where we might be.

But the huge misconception in that statement of faith is that we don't have to prepare. Nothing could be further from the truth. God demands the best from us, and we cannot give God our best without preparation. Jesus prepared by spending forty days in the wilderness. Paul prepared at the home of Cornelius. Moses prepared as he made his way back to Egypt from his encounter with God at the burning bush. Even though God calls us and equips us, it is our duty and responsibility to prepare—prayerfully, carefully, diligently, faithfully—to proclaim God's Word. Anything less is a travesty.

Let me give you an analogy that I've used a few times. Suppose (heaven forbid) you had a brain tumor, and a friend of yours who had never studied medicine of any kind offered to operate on your brain. Your friend said simply, "Don't worry. God will guide my hands as I open your skull and operate on your brain." Would you trust your friend? Or would you prefer to have a doctor who had studied diligently and prepared faithfully for years and years do the surgery? All right; it is an extreme example. But that friend was going to operate on your mortal brain; when we preach, we are touching people's immortal souls. That demands our best and most prayerful preparation.

Starting When?

One of the questions beginning preachers always ask is, "When do I start working on a sermon?" After all, if you are assigned to preach to a congregation on a regular basis, even if it is for only a few successive Sundays, you are faced with preparing a new sermon every 168 hours. When do you start?

Almost everyone who preaches has her or his own unique approach. No one way is right or wrong, but I can tell you when I start. I often read next Sunday's lectionary passages before I leave the church after worship on a Sunday morning. (I don't read them before this Sunday morning's worship, since I would begin thinking about next week's selections instead of this Sunday's sermon.) Then I try to devote some time Sunday afternoon to thinking about those lections so that by suppertime I have in mind the general focus of next Sunday's sermon and have made tentative plans about which of the Scripture readings will be the emphasis of my sermon. I also have in mind a rough general idea of where I want to go with that sermon; in other words, the main thrust of the sermon.

This approach came from some excellent advice I received in my first year of seminary many years ago. Our homiletics (the study of preaching) professor said, "Select your texts as early in the week as possible; then brood about them all during the week."

I've always been fascinated with the word *brood*. What it means in this case is to keep those lections and the thrust of that sermon in your mind all week long, to think about it at any moment you can, to reflect on it as you are driving, falling asleep, doing some shopping, almost anything. It's almost as if those Scripture passages are the lenses through which you see that entire week. The texts are never out of your mind. You are letting them fill your consciousness, saturate your thinking, literally get inside of you. Remember when I wrote of spending that day thinking about a single New Testament verse during that New Testament study? That's what happens when you brood about those lections all week long. They become part of you, and the God who makes those texts is alive in you.

This doesn't mean that I stick with that first focus or thrust I came up with on Sunday afternoon. By Tuesday or Wednesday I've often changed what I want to do with those texts several times as they have grown within me. I like to think that the Holy Spirit is working as I mull over those texts all week, that the Holy Spirit is giving direction and guidance to what I am to say to God's people this coming Sunday about the good news.

But What If…?

Yes, I know that you will not always have the luxury of a full week to prepare a sermon. Lay speakers get called on short notice, maybe as little as twelve hours (although I hope that would not happen to an inexperienced lay speaker). But the principle still holds. Get those lections in mind and think about them, concentrate on them, every moment you have.

Remember how the Israelites were instructed in Deuteronomy to keep the words of the Law before them at all times, speaking of them as they went about their way, binding them as a sign on their hands, fixing them on their foreheads, and writing them on the doorposts of their houses (Deuteronomy 6:4-9)? Well, that is the way you ought to live with those texts as you prepare to preach. Even if you have only a few hours, get them inside of you. Live with them and let them live with you.

Most of the rest of the suggestions in this chapter are modeled on a week to prepare for a sermon. If you don't have a week, the suggestions are still relevant. Simply compress the time, but do not omit any of the steps if you can possibly avoid doing so.

What Else Besides Brooding?

You are absolutely right; thinking about, brooding over, those lections is only the beginning of your preparation. You will want to undertake a number of additional steps before you begin to put your ideas down on paper for that sermon coming up in just six and a half days.

Monday

Yesterday afternoon you read all the lections, perhaps several times over. You can recall the gist of each of them easily. But now begins the serious study. Reread those lections in as many different translations of the Bible as you can. Include some paraphrases if you'd like, such as the J. B. Phillips' paraphrase of the New Testament; but be sure you read and study those texts in reputable translations.

What's the difference between a translation (or version) and a paraphrase? While the difference includes many technical details, this is the primary difference:

- A *translation* (such as the New Revised Standard Version, the New International Version, or the Contemporary English Version, to name just three) is prepared by a panel of scholars using the most ancient manuscripts available. These experts translate the original Hebrew and Greek as carefully as possible, keeping all of the nuances of the original language.
- A *paraphrase*, on the other hand, is most often the work of one individual. This person takes any translation she or he prefers and seeks to put that translation into her or his own words. The paraphraser makes little or no attempt to uncover the original meanings of the texts. Her or his goal is to create a readable edition of the Bible by substituting her or his simpler words and sentence constructions for those in the versions of the Bible she or he is paraphrasing.

You are correct; because a paraphraser is most often working alone and her or his goal is readability, often the paraphraser's own opinions, perspectives, biases, and ideas creep into the paraphrase. This is not always negative, but it results in a Bible that is less true to the original than is a translation.

As you read, jot down words that give you pause. You may know full well what those words mean, but what is their impact in these texts? Look up these words in your concordance; see how they are used in other biblical passages. Jot down questions about the texts you would like to ask the biblical writers, if you could.

Pay special attention to the ways the translations and versions vary from one another. How does the word selection in one translation illuminate the meaning of the text? Perhaps the lections are easier to understand by piecing together words and phrases from several different translations.

And here's a hint for the lection taken from the Gospel: Consult *Gospel Parallels,* a special book that lines up the Gospels side by side so that you can see how Matthew, Mark, and Luke tell the same stories but in slightly different ways. Quite possibly, one of your study Bibles will have a harmony of the Gospels among the study aids. This resource does the same thing as the *Gospel Parallels,* but it usually does it by chapter and verse rather than by printing the entire text.

Next, be sure you understand the context of each of the passages. This means you'll have to read several chapters of the Scriptures that precede and follow each of the texts. Think about questions such as these:

- Where was Jesus when he said these words?
- To whom was Jesus talking?
- Was Jesus addressing believers or nonbelievers?
- Was this early or late in Jesus' ministry?
- Where did Jesus say these words: in Galilee, in Jerusalem, or in Samaria?

Now, jot down tentative answers to these questions about the texts:

- What does this text say?
- What did this text mean to its original hearers or readers?
- What does this text say to us; that is, how can this text be applied in our time?
- And to be sure you really understand these texts, write your own paraphrase of each one. Try it first without looking at the Scriptures. (How well do you remember each text?) Then go back and rewrite that paraphrase using the biblical passage as a guide.

Tuesday

Still brooding about those texts? Good. The serious study continues. Now is the time to dig into those Bible dictionaries and commentaries, to pull out that atlas, and to do some hard comparative work in the concordance.

Look up the names of people and places in your Bible dictionary. If you're dealing with people, get their relationships with other biblical characters straight. For example: Was Abner on Saul's side or on David's side? Was John Mark the missionary Paul rejected, or was that someone else?

Check the names of places using your atlas. Was this place in Israel or Judah (if it's an Old Testament site), or in Galilee or Judea or Samaria (if it's a New Testament site)? Try to understand distances in the biblical world. Remember that although the part of Palestine that figures prominently in the Bible is only a little more than one hundred miles in length, travel was difficult and seldom direct.

Do you have people and places fairly straight in your head? Good. Now dig into those commentaries. Remember to consult at least two commentaries in addition to the footnotes in your Bible. Read not only what the commentators say about the texts themselves but also what the contexts of those texts say. Keep asking these questions: How are these commentaries alike? How are they different? What does each one emphasize in each text? What does each suggest is the point of each text? And, most importantly, what can I conclude is the most important element in each of these texts?

Clue: Don't be at all surprised if your understanding of these texts changes drastically as a result of your commentary, dictionary, and concordance study. This means you're letting the text and its meanings seep into you; you're opening yourself to the text; and you're willing to keep an open mind and change some long-held notions about some of the texts. This is growth, the sanctifying grace of God at work in you.

Now do some preliminary sketching of the major points in the lections you've been studying, especially as these apply to contemporary life. Remember, you are called to proclaim the good news of the gospel of Jesus Christ and to lift up and glorify Christ, our Lord. This means that all of this diligent study is ultimately aimed at this purpose. Your study is not undertaken so that you can impress your hearers with your erudition or understanding; it is not intended to amaze them with your knowledge of the Scriptures; it is not designed to make you seem to be in possession of information your hearers do not have. To do any of these would be to make you, not the gospel of Christ, the focal point of the sermon.

No, your study and concentration, all of your brooding, is intended only to equip you to proclaim the gospel of Jesus Christ as effectively, as clearly, as engagingly as possible.

6

GET READY—II

Knowing the Congregation

You're on your way. You've studied the lections for the Sunday you will preach. You've read the Scripture passages in several different translations; looked up difficult words, names, and places in the Bible dictionary; located the scenes of events on the maps in your Bible atlas; and checked out a harmony of the Gospels to see how the gospel story reads in each Gospel in which it appears.

And you're still brooding about those texts, letting them seep within you. But now your brooding is beginning to take some shape and some directions, for the sermon is starting to form in your mind.

You have another large element to consider as you begin the detailed preparation of the sermon: To whom will you be preaching?

It Worked Before

Once in a while a preacher will say, "It doesn't matter to whom I'll be preaching. It's a great sermon. It went over well the last time I preached it, so I'll preach it again here."

More often than not, that approach just doesn't work; that is, more often than you'd care to imagine, a sermon that went really well in one congregation goes nowhere in another congregation. Points and illustrations that really got through in one setting seem to fall flat in another setting. And the preacher who relies on that sermon barrel (his or her file of old sermons) is in for some disappointments.

Why? Because each congregation is different, unique, special. One size does not fit all. The presentation of the gospel of Jesus Christ must be new and fresh in each congregation, and the presentation must be geared for that particular congregation—and no other—in so far as possible.

I learned this the hard way many years ago when I was invited to preach one Sunday at a church in a neighboring small town. I knew little about the town, other than that it was in a rural setting. And I guessed that many of the members of the congregation would be older, probably rural, people. I went to the file and pulled out a sermon that had worked well in another rural setting of older people. I thought, *I'll just dust this one off and head out there and preach it again.*

What I failed to learn before going to the church that morning was that the small community was the site of a military boarding school for high school students, both girls and boys. This was the church that most of that student body attended each Sunday morning, attired in their dress military uniforms.

You can imagine my surprise when I walked into the church and found, sitting in the center of a handful of middle-age and older people in the congregation, about seventy-five starched and earnest young faces in neat rows. I learned later that almost all these students were from other states and that many of them had not seen a family member in months. They were as old as eighteen and as young as thirteen, and their needs and interests were not the needs and interests of rural older adults.

I tried on the spot to adapt the sermon I had planned for the older people so that it would be relevant for these young men and women; but it didn't work. The cadets were polite, attentive, and gracious; however, I did not speak to them the gospel of Jesus Christ in a form that captured their imagination and enthusiasm. That sermon failed because I had not taken the time to learn something about the congregation to whom I would be preaching that Sunday.

Never again.

So, Ask

What do you need to know about the members of a congregation before you participate in worship with them and preach to them? How do you get what you need to know? Good questions, but let's get things in sequence here.

Remember our fictitious, rather ideal scenario in the last chapter? Part of our scenario was that you would contact the person who creates the worship bulletin and tell him or her your sermon title and suggested hymns. We said you would do that on Tuesday evening.

Great, from a couple of standpoints:

1. By Tuesday night you have considered the lections and have a good idea of where you want to go with your sermon.
2. The person who does the bulletin probably knows as much about the congregation as anyone else. Chances are that this person has been in that congregation longer than the current pastor has been there.

So, you call the person who prepares the bulletin. (You did tell the pastor who invited you to preach that you would be contacting that person, didn't you? That's how you got the name and telephone number. And if all has gone well, the pastor has told him or her that you'd be calling.)

You call and, after making small talk for a moment, tell the Scripture texts you want read as part of the service, the Scripture you will read just before the sermon, and the title of your sermon.

A Quick Comment About Sermon Titles

Many preachers labor more over the sermon title than they do over the text of the sermon itself. These preachers are often aiming for a cute, clever, or catchy sermon title, something that will grab people and make them want to listen. The problem with this approach to sermon titles is that the sermon often fails to live up to the cleverness of the title, and the congregation feels let down.

Descriptive sermon titles are much better than clever ones. And if the truth be known, people don't remember sermon titles; but they do remember the content (or lack of content) of the sermon. Many people have come up to me and said something such as, "Remember that sermon you preached on the wise men about a year ago?" Never has someone come up and said, "Remember the Epiphany sermon you preached titled 'Find Him Yourself, Herod?'" Don't labor over titles. Use a fragment of a verse or a descriptive phrase as a sermon title. Titles such as "Grace Unlimited" or "Follow Me" say more than "When Your Dipstick Comes Up Dry" or "Don't Rock the Boat, Zebedee."

Leave the cutesy titles for others. Stick to the basics. If you're spending more than five minutes on a sermon title, you're spending too much time. (No one said that a sermon had to have a title. If the person who does the bulletin simply wants to list "The Sermon" or "The Message," fine.

You will also want to select the hymns you'd like to use in the service of worship. Remember to use a good strong hymn of praise and thanksgiving to open the worship, a hymn of commitment and discipleship to close the worship, and a hymn somewhat tied to the theme of your sermon following the sermon.

Here's a hint I've learned the hard way: Pick two or three hymns for each spot so that you have backups. Be prepared with alternatives, since the person who is preparing the bulletin is likely to say about one of your suggestions, "We sang that last Sunday" or, "We don't know that hymn."

Now you're ready to raise some questions about the congregation. Start off with something informal, such as, "Could I ask you a couple questions about the people who come to worship in your church?" Then continue with some factual questions:

- How many people come to Sunday worship?
- Are most of them regular in attendance?
- What's the age span? Are they mostly young couples? older people? families? or what? About how many teenagers attend worship? How many children attend on an average Sunday?

Now ask some of the more in-depth kinds of questions:

- Are most of the people in worship church members?
- Did most of them grow up as United Methodists or as part of the Methodist family of denominations? If not, what are some of the denominations represented in the congregation?
- Are many of the people in the congregation related? (In some small-membership congregations, the majority of those in attendance may be members of two or three extended families that have intermarried over the generations. In my first student appointment, more than half the congregation was named Jones. I had to leave behind one of my favorite expressions: "Keeping up with the Joneses.")

Another cluster of questions might concern what these people do:

- Are most of the people in your church farmers? Or do they work at the big plant on the edge of your town? Or do you have a mix of schoolteachers, doctors, merchants, and other kinds of occupations?
- How many retirees are in the congregation? (Yes, there is a difference in preaching to working people and to retirees. My last appointment had a small handful of retirees. My present appointment is near a beautiful lake known for its recreational use. Consequently, my congregation is filled with active, comparatively young retirees who golf, fish, bowl, boat, and stay busy.)

You'll want to move into areas that have to do with our Christian faith:

- Do most of the people in your congregation know the Bible fairly well? (If yes, then you can refer to the story of the good Samaritan, and most people will know what you're describing. If no, then you may need to retell the story of the good Samaritan quickly if it's part of your sermon.)
- Would you describe your congregation as theologically conservative, liberal, middle-of-the-road, or what?

Another helpful question concerns special ministries of the congregation. Knowing if the congregation is proud of its missions ministry, its youth group, its music program, its United Methodist Women organization, or its social outreach ministry, for example, can be helpful.

You'll think of additional important questions to raise, and you'll be surprised at the additional information you'll hear about the congregation. All of it will be invaluable as you begin your intensive sermon preparation.

For example, I was asked to preach for four Sundays at a church with which I was not at all familiar. I telephoned one of the laity and asked questions much like those listed here. Near the end of our conversation, the church member said, "Maybe I should tell you about Billy." I replied that I'd be happy to hear about Billy.

She told me Billy was a much-loved member of the congregation who was in his mid-thirties. He attended all church events with his parents, for Billy had a rather serious mental impairment. She said that Billy loved to sing and would often start singing loudly at inopportune times, including during the sermon. The congregation ignored Billy's songs; they had known Billy for years and loved him. But Billy's spontaneous music could be disconcerting for a visiting preacher.

I met Billy as I entered the church that next Sunday, and I quickly grew to love his gentle and honest ways. Sure enough, he broke out into song in the middle of my first sermon there; but since I had been forewarned, I just continued on with the message. Billy and I became fast friends, as did everyone who ever met Billy.

What is the point of all this? Simply this: We must know our congregation, the people to whom we will be preaching, if we are going to be effective in our proclamation of the message. Canned or prepackaged sermons do not work because, as I said before, one size does not fit all. In fact, that one size often fits nobody.

So, trying to preach a sermon you heard once is a futile effort. That sermon you heard may have touched you deeply—and thank God it did—but that does not mean you can duplicate it with an entirely different congregation and have the same results. To believe otherwise is to demonstrate a lack of respect for the congregation to whom you will be preaching and a lack of understanding of the uniqueness that God has created in each of us.

All This Information

You've gathered quite a bit of information about this congregation for whom you will be preaching in a few short days. Try to get that information organized in some way that makes it manageable for you.

I try to jot down a profile of the congregation based on what I heard. That profile is usually a paragraph in length and contains the major characteristics of the congregation that I learned from my conversations. The profile becomes my target audience; that is, the congregation for whom I am preparing this sermon.

A profile might look something like this:

> The fifty or so worshipers on a typical Sunday at Wesley Church are mostly members of four extended families, who have farmed in this area for several generations and who have always been part of the Methodist connection. Since Bible study has always been strong in this congregation, most of the worshipers know the Scriptures quite well. Though the church is small in membership, it includes a strong youth group; and as many as eight to ten of the worshipers on Sunday may be teenagers. The church has had a variety of relatively short-term pastors, so they are comfortable with a variety of perspectives on theology.

I find it important to write that profile out, often in large letters, and keep it before me as I'm working on the sermon. Even though we are proclaiming God's Word and God is the center of the sermon, we are proclaiming that Word to people. We must keep those people in mind constantly.

Keep Them in Mind

Keeping those people in mind means several things:
- proclaiming the gospel in such a way that it speaks to the life situations of those in the congregation (One professor of preaching liked to say, "Scratch them where they, not you, itch.");
- proclaiming the gospel in a vocabulary and style that is understandable to those who are listening (Compound and complex sentences with a college-level vocabulary is expected in some settings; in other settings such constructions would turn people off completely.);
- proclaiming the gospel in ways that relate to experiences the listeners have had or are having;
- proclaiming the gospel using illustrations drawn from the lives of the listeners, not from the lives of people remote from those listeners (This is why we often experience the shepherd images from the Bible being restated in contemporary images, for few of us have had experiences as a shepherd or herdsman.);

- proclaiming the gospel at the level of your hearers' theological understanding (Waxing eloquently about your comprehension of soteriology may be impressive; but if you are speaking to new Christians, your eloquence may be far removed from where they are in their understanding of the Christian faith.);
- proclaiming the gospel in such a way that all that you do and say from the pulpit shows the utmost respect for your hearers and their life situations (It is exactly at this point that many preachers fail, for those preachers see themselves as an authority figure dictating to those who need instruction. Such a perspective does not respect the hearers, and the hearers sense that they are not being respected. A preacher is a member of the worshiping congregation, and just as each member of the congregation has a role to play in the corporate worship, so does the preacher have a role to play. The preacher's role is no more or no less important than the roles of others in the community at worship.);
- proclaiming the gospel in such a way that each member of the congregation is recognized and affirmed as a child of God. We cannot do that unless we know something about the members of that congregation.

What are some other things that occur to you as you focus on keeping the congregation in mind during your sermon preparation time?

7
GET READY—III

The Nuts and Bolts of Sermon Preparation

Are you ready to go? It's late Tuesday evening or sometime on Wednesday. You've been brooding since Sunday afternoon about those lections, the Scripture passages that make up this coming Sunday's worship service. You've dug into the Bible study helps, both in your study Bibles and in outside resource books. You think you have a good grip on those passages.

In plain sight there on your desk is the profile of the congregation to which you will be preaching on Sunday morning. Go ahead, make some changes in that profile. It's for your eyes only. If you recall something else that was said in the telephone conversation, include it in the profile.

So, you know the Scriptures and you know the congregation. Now comes the fascinating and frightening step: writing the sermon.

Write a Sermon

Yes, that word is *write*, which means you need to compose that sermon word by word, sentence by sentence, and paragraph by paragraph. You need to write a full manuscript of that sermon. In truth, you will write several full manuscripts of that sermon as you continue to work.

Some experienced preachers seldom write full manuscripts. But notice a key word in that sentence: *experienced.* Unless you have many years of preaching under your belt, then you (and I) need to write a full manuscript.

This chapter is going to take you through a sequence of steps in preparing a full manuscript for your sermon. You may be tempted to skip some steps or to try to do a couple steps at the same time. But I urge you as you begin preaching to follow these steps carefully until you're secure in sermon writing, until you can combine steps and still proclaim the gospel of Jesus Christ with the best that's in you.

A Word About Length

Before you actually begin writing, I want to say a couple things about the length of your sermon and therefore of your manuscript. And I make these comments out of my own experience.

After my first year in seminary, before I had taken any formal courses in homiletics (preaching), I was asked to preach for a vacationing pastor in a town about ninety miles from where I was spending the summer. I had never preached before, but I jumped at the opportunity and then felt an absolute, stark terror.

I took an afternoon off, without pay, from my summer job so that I could get started on the sermon. Fortified by a big lunch, I headed for the local library because I wanted somewhere quiet to work: no telephones, no temptation to switch on the television or the stereo, no interruptions. I could simply write the sermon that had been percolating in the back of my mind for some time.

I started writing. And I wrote. And I wrote. And I wrote some more. Pleased with my longhand manuscript, I ran home and furiously spent the rest of the evening typing out that manuscript. It came to twenty-four single-spaced, type-written pages. Do you have any idea how long preaching such a sermon would require? Literally hours.

Realizing that my sermon was a little long, I read it over, this time critically rather than appreciatively. I discovered that I had crammed everything I knew about everything into that one sermon. I had used every clever illustration I had ever read or heard, employed every cliché that came to mind, and quoted all the Scripture I knew—and some I didn't know. The result was absolute gibberish.

Back to the drawing board...

I made some inquiries, checked some resources, and found that the average sermon runs between fifteen and twenty minutes in length. (Indeed, the average person listening to a sermon has a serious lapse of attention about every seven minutes.) Some more checking revealed that about two and a half to three minutes are required to preach a single double-spaced, typewritten page of manuscript. (You can read faster than that, but you cannot preach faster than that and expect your hearers to get anything from your message.) That means that a good length for a manuscript is about five to eight double-spaced, typewritten (or computer generated) pages.

Yes, I know you're going to say you're just getting warmed up in five to eight pages. But you're not preaching for you; you're preaching for and to that congregation, and they begin to turn off a preacher after twenty minutes, no matter how well she or he is preaching.

So, set as an outside goal an eight-page double-spaced manuscript. You can't tell a congregation everything you know in that amount of time, but you're not supposed to.

Zeroing In

All of this means, then, that you need to focus your sermon tightly. You've been thinking about, brooding about, those texts for many hours now. You have a good understanding of the congregation to whom you'll be preaching.

Now answer this question before putting pen to paper: What is the main point with which you want people to walk away after this sermon? What is the main point you want to make in this sermon?

That's right: *Point, singular.*

The old rule about a sermon consisting of three points and a poem has long ago been put to rest. In fact, that approach may have reflected a lack of confidence in the ability to make any point. If the preacher throws three points out there, one might click with some of the people in the congregation. Try this yourself: Can you remember hearing a multiple-point sermon recently? Can you recall all of the points of that sermon? Perhaps you can, but more often than not we're captured by one of the three points, remember that point, and forget or overlook the other points in the traditional three-points-and-a-poem format.

But an even more important reason to build your sermon around a single point is that you are a beginning preacher. Perhaps someone with years and years of experience can pull off complex, multiple-point sermons. But until you have years of experience in writing sermon manuscripts under your belt, stick with a single point. And make that point effectively.

A good, solid, single-point sermon is like the old cliché about writing and teaching: "You tell them what you're going to tell them; then you tell them; and then you tell them what you've told them." In other words, in preaching, making a single point in several different ways is more effective than what I tried to do with my first sermon: telling them everything I thought I knew.

Additionally, a good, strong, single-point sermon keeps your listeners focused. Why? Because you are focused. We lose our hearers when our sermon wanders all over the countryside; we hold them when we are making a single point directly, powerfully, passionately.

From where does that single point come? You're exactly right: from your brooding over those lections, from your study of those lections, from your living intimately with those lections over several days. That central point, that main thrust of those lections has emerged and grown in your thinking, and now it is ready to blossom. It may or may not be the main point of these lectionary passages as identified by some of your commentary study. It may be a point that suddenly hit you when you least expected it, perhaps when you were studying or when you were going about other activities. And it may not be the main point that is usually stressed with these passages. You have tried to let the Scriptures speak to you, and you have listened and heard. Now let them speak through you.

Here is one of many possible examples of catching a new point or twist on a familiar passage: In the story of the good Samaritan (Luke 10), the story is told in response to the lawyer's question, "Who is my neighbor?" At the end of the story, Jesus asks the lawyer, "Which of these...was a neighbor to the man who fell into the hands of the robbers?" When Jesus posed the question this way, he made the lawyer identify with the man who fell among thieves, not with the Samaritan. A twist on this story is that even while we seek to help others, we must be open to the help and ministry of others when we are in need. Our neighbor is the one who comes to us when we are broken, frightened, and alone. That's hard for many of us to do because we like to think we've got it all together and don't need anyone else's help. Seeing the two clear meanings in the story of the good Samaritan answers that emphatically.

And before you get too far along in your preparation with that point you've developed so carefully, ask yourself the crucial question that we brought up way back in the first chapter: Does this point proclaim and emphasize the good news of the gospel? Does it glorify Jesus Christ? If you can't honestly answer yes to questions such as these, then you'd better do some more study and redevelop your central point.

Preaching is first and always the proclamation of the good news of the gospel of Jesus Christ. Let nothing divert you from that fundamental fact.

I've Got a Point; Now What?

You've zeroed in on the point you want to make in your sermon. Good. You've written it down in several different ways to make sure it's a good, clear point. If possible, try writing it the first time with God as the subject of the sentence and a second time with human beings as the subject of the sentence. A quick example: Let's suppose you were preaching on the parables about the lost in Luke, chapter 15. Write a simple point first with God, then with us, as the subject: God (*subject*) seeks and saves those who are lost. We (*subject*) may be lost and not even be aware of being lost.

You've got your point. You've looked at it from several different angles. Now you're ready to develop it into a sermon.

A Series of Questions

The development of your sermon starts with a series of questions. These questions may vary according to the biblical texts you are using in your sermon and your central point, but these basic questions can be adapted to fit your situation.

1. How does my point emerge from the Scripture texts? How do these texts lead directly to this point? (A word of warning: If you can't honestly answer these questions, you may need to look at the Scriptures and at your point again. You may be on the verge of preaching your own ideas rather than preaching the Scriptures.)

2. Why is this point important to the people to whom I will be preaching?

3. What do my hearers need to know and understand before they can get this point? (This is the place for biblical background, if necessary. For example, who were the Samaritans? In the Book of Ruth, what did Boaz mean by the right of redemption? Why was Jesus' encounter with the woman at the well in John 4 unusual in terms of where it happened and when [time of day] it happened?)

4. How does the point that emerges from the Scriptures relate to the lives of the people to whom I am preaching? And a related question: Do I need to make the connection for them, or is the connection so obvious that I need only to create the opportunity for that connection to be made in the minds and hearts of the hearers?

5. How can I illustrate or give examples of this point that tie the biblical texts to contemporary life?

As always, jotting down answers to these questions will assist you as you begin writing your sermon. So, keep the questions and your responses in front of you as you work on the sermon. (Yes, you're keeping several things before you as you write, but each of them is important. To forget or neglect any of them is inviting less than your best as you prepare your sermon.)

Last Thing Before You Start Writing

You've done good preliminary work. You're set to go. But I'd suggest one more task before you begin writing the manuscript for your sermon. If you are anything like I was when I was in school, you hated these exercises. But they have proven over the years to be invaluable.

Develop an outline of your sermon before you begin to write the manuscript. You remember how to do an outline:

- Your main point is the title of your outline.
- Your introduction or beginning is *1* or *A* or Roman numeral *I.* (Those details really don't matter.) Under this introduction, list the subpoints you want to make in the introduction in the order you want to make them.
- Now for the development of your point. This development might be in two or three steps, with subpoints under each step. Sure, you can have subpoints to your subpoints. Don't be afraid to go for detail in the outline.

Watch the sequence carefully.

- Where and when do you introduce biblical background?
- Where and how do you define theological terms with which some in the congregation may not be familiar?
- Where and how do you use illustrations or examples? While illustrations and examples are not exactly subpoints, include them in your outline. For example, sometimes you will want to use an example before you make a subpoint, in order to set up the subpoint. At other times, you will want to make a subpoint and then illustrate it with an example. Want some examples? Read Jesus' parables. He used both of these approaches.
- And finally, your conclusion is the last part of your outline. It too will have several subpoints; list these carefully.

A word of warning: A conclusion is not a summary; it is not a simple retelling of the entire sermon in a sentence or two. To do so leaves the congregation wondering why you didn't just give them the two sentences at the beginning. A conclusion is the logical development of the sermon that leads to fixing the main point of the sermon in the minds and hearts of those listeners.

Here's a suggestion: Be patient and gentle with yourself. You will tear up several complete outlines before you're happy with one. You will start several outlines and not even get beyond the second point before you realize these outlines are not going to work. Don't get frustrated. Instead, congratulate yourself that you are taking this responsibility seriously and that you are giving it your best. Seldom do any of us do our best work on the first try. That goes for almost all facets of life, including sermon writing.

Start Writing

Now do it. Write a full—and I mean full, complete, every word—manuscript. Write it by hand, if you wish, or use a typewriter or computer. But write out a full manuscript including the Scripture passages you plan to quote, the illustrations or examples you plan to use, and so forth. This is the only way you can determine if you are preparing a balanced sermon.

By *balance* I mean a sermon that gives a proportionate amount of time to introduction, development, and conclusion. I've heard sermons that had fifteen minutes of introduction, with five minutes left for development and conclusion. Some sermons will need longer introductions; others will need little or no introduction (an Easter sermon, for example).

Occasionally, a conclusion can be one sentence, as in the form of a challenge, an imperative, or an invitation. At other times, the conclusion may be lengthier, drawing together what may have seemed like several disparate ideas into a cohesive whole. But only by writing a full manuscript of that sermon will you know if you have achieved balance or not.

As you write this manuscript, do not be overly concerned about length. You're going to do some heavy editing on this manuscript or, more likely, go through several rewrites before you have a workable manuscript. Spend your writing time on putting together a cohesive, well-structured, simple, and direct message that conveys the point you want to make by engaging your listeners with a winsome introduction and leaving them with a challenging conclusion.

I can almost guarantee one of two things about this first manuscript: It will either be much, much longer than you expected it would be, or it will be much, much shorter than you anticipated it would be. But again, don't worry about that. You will have time to rework and rework that manuscript until you have it the way you want it.

Good. You just finished writing your first manuscript for your sermon. Now, get up and leave it right where it is. Walk away from it. Go do something else. Right now your mind is exhausted. You've done good work, but you're not ready to reread that sermon now. Give yourself a well-earned break. And when you come back to start the editing and refining process, you'll be sharper and more incisive as you make the changes that will help you proclaim the gospel of Jesus Christ.

8

THE KING'S ENGLISH

The Need for Good Grammar, Style, and Word Selection

I couldn't believe it. The first time I heard it I thought it must be a mistake. But now the preacher had said it for the fourth time in a matter of just a couple minutes. I cringed, not wanting to hear what I was hearing. But he said it again. And this preacher was supposed to be a college and seminary graduate. How could he say it over and over again?

He started out by saying something such as this: "Our New Testament Scripture is from Revelations 3, verses 14 through 22." After reading the verses, he said, "Here ends the reading from Revelations."

The sermon began, "In chapters 2 and 3 of Revelations, John addresses seven churches, churches that are similar to churches in our time. This message from Revelations speaks to us, too."

By then, I'm ashamed to say, I had tuned him out. If he didn't care any more than that, was no more careful than that in his sermon preparation, then I had to wonder about his credibility. I suspect many in the congregation did so also.

(What was the problem, you ask? Check the name of the last book in your Bible.)

I thought I'd heard everything, but I hadn't.

Quite some time later I visited a congregation in another city. This congregation numbered several hundred members, and the pastor was a seminary graduate with an advanced degree. His text was a fascinating story, the story of David and Bathsheba from 2 Samuel, chapters 11 and 12. The preacher did not dwell long on the details of David's sin. Good; that is not the point of this story.

But then the preacher came to Nathan's criticism of David and began to tell Nathan's story of the rich man and the poor man. As he described the poor man, the preacher reported that the man had nothing but a little ewe lamb. However, that's not what I heard, for the preacher, there in front of his congregation, said that the poor man had one little "e-wee" lamb. I wondered, *Is this preacher trying to be funny?* I thought he was, so I chuckled silently to myself.

But he said it a second, a third, and a fourth time. He kept pronouncing *ewe* as *e-wee* with absolute seriousness. How could I or anyone else take this preacher seriously after a repeated gaff like that? (Of course, you know that a female sheep is pronounced as if it were spelled *you*, not *e-wee*.)

What is the point of all this? Simply this: Proclaiming the gospel of Jesus Christ demands your best, the absolute best you can provide. And that means if you don't know the name of a biblical book or how to pronounce a word correctly, look it up until you do. Your whole sermon can lose its effectiveness and the entire congregation can turn you off in an instant if you demonstrate sloppy preparation by pretending you know how to pronounce a word when indeed you don't. (I'm not talking about Old Testament names here. See the additional information in the gray box on page 65.) You have no excuse for mispronouncing an English word or even a fairly common name or geographic location.

For example, have you ever heard someone pronounce the name of the state in which the city of Chicago is found as *Illinoise?* Wrong. Wrong. Wrong. Or totally butchered a common English word? "This is true irregardless of what happens." Friends, *irregardless* is nonstandard speech and should not be used. Instead, use *irrespective* or *regardless.*

How can you avoid these errors? When you are not absolutely certain, sure, and confident of the pronunciation of a word, look it up. Learn how to use the dictionary (remember, you learned back in school). Check and recheck yourself. A moment spent verifying the pronunciation of a word now will save you snickers, chuckles, embarrassment, and a tarnished proclamation of the gospel.

Again, what's the point of all this? Simply this: Few things will impeach your preaching, destroy your credibility, and lose your listeners more quickly than the sloppy use of language and grammar.

Biblical names, both of people and of places, can give anyone fits. One of the problems is that even the best scholars aren't sure just how some Old Testament names are pronounced because biblical Hebrew was written without vowels until after the birth of Jesus. Jewish scribes (called Masoretes) tried to ensure the purity of the Hebrew text by inserting what have come to be called vowel points. (Imagine the consonants of a first name Tm without any vowels. Is this pronounced Tom, Tim, Tam, or what? This was the case with some of the ancient Hebrew names.)

However, we do have what we might call generally accepted pronunciations of biblical names. Preachers will avoid confusing their congregations if they stick to some of these. How do you know what these pronunciations are? Many Bibles print names broken into syllables with pronunciation suggestions. But one of the best sources is a little book titled *The HarperCollins Bible Pronunciation Guide* (Harper San Francisco, 1989).

I had a Bible professor in seminary who was from the Netherlands and had written extensively and was recognized as a world-renowned Bible scholar. He caught us off guard one day when he referred to the Book of Nee-HUH-mi-uh in the Old Testament. When someone in the class said, "Isn't that pronounced Nee-huh-MI-uh, he said that in Europe the book was pronounced his way, and that scholars simply have no way of knowing exact Old Testament pronunciations.

That Word Again

I used a word that many of us don't like to hear: *grammar.* Many of us didn't much care for the study of grammar back in school. Because we could communicate effectively with our friends without worrying about the rules of grammar, we thought grammar rules were useless.

But the rules of grammar are absolutely crucial to preaching and to proclaiming the gospel of Jesus Christ. Clear mistakes in grammar, especially repeated mistakes, communicate to our listeners that we don't know or, worse, that we don't care. Preaching demands our best in every way, and that makes us obligated to present our sermons in as nearly perfect grammar as we can. Anything less is not worthy of the pulpit.

A couple years ago, I taught a class in one of our United Methodist seminaries. Among the course requirements I gave the students were several written assignments. When the written assignments were submitted, I was appalled at the quality of the grammar displayed in many of them. When I devoted about thirty minutes of class time on one occasion to pointing out serous grammatical errors and arguing for the importance of solid, correct grammar, I was met with rather heated criticisms. One student said, "You know what I meant. What difference does it make that my grammar was a little sloppy?" Another student said, "You're not here to teach us grammar; that's old stuff, anyway."

Wrong.

The ability to communicate clearly, directly, and effectively is one of the most important characteristics any preacher or anyone who would proclaim the good news of the gospel can possess. And, fortunately, we can learn that characteristic if we are willing to be diligent. Almost everything we do within a congregation—teaching Sunday school, participating in the church council, even witnessing to a friend—depends on our ability to communicate effectively. And the rules of grammar enable us to communicate effectively and clearly. Those rules are not there to trip us; they are there to enable us to use the English language effectively.

So, what do you do if you're uncertain about grammar? Just slide over it? Or figure that if it sounds right to you, it must be right? Absolutely not.

The proclamation of the good news demands your best, so unless you are unmistakably sure of the rules of grammar as you write your sermon manuscript—absolutely certain that your grammar is impeccable—please, please ask someone else to read over your manuscript and to point out the grammatical mistakes.

Who? Do you know a high school or college English teacher? a journalist, such as a newspaper writer? a book or magazine editor or a copy editor? Ask that person to read over your manuscript and to do two things:

• First, mark and correct any errors in grammar.
• Second, and even more important, show you your mistakes in grammar and give you the rule or principle for each error so that you won't make the mistake again.

For example: "Give your child what they need to grow as Christians." Grammatical error? Yes. *Child* is singular, so the pronoun referring to *child* must be singular. That means that the *they* is incorrect and needs to be replaced with *she or he* (the *or* makes this a singular construction), or the sentence needs to be recast to something such as: "Give your children what they need."

Make sure that you understand each error your reader cites and how to correct it. Yes, grammar is a bunch of rules, and few people can remember all of them. But they are the rules of clear, concise, precise communication. They are the rules that prevent your message from being misunderstood. They are the rules that mark your sermon as the best you can do.

What Does That Word Mean?

Along with poor pronunciation and bad grammar, another element that can doom your sermon from the start is poor choice of words or plain misuse of words.

A sermon need not be filled with big or complicated words; simple, direct words communicate more effectively. I have heard many sermons literally fall apart because the preacher tried to use words with which she or he was unfamiliar. Even though the preacher may pronounce a word correctly, if that word is not a natural part of her or his vocabulary, that word's use in a sermon can lead to the sermon's downfall.

The choice of words can suggest several things to a congregation. The use of large, complex words when simple words will do suggests that the preacher is trying more to impress members of the congregation with his or her wisdom than to communicate the gospel. I once heard a preacher talking about the "intermediate eventualities of specified courses or patterns of personal behavior" when he could just as well have talked about the results or consequences of actions. Who was he trying to impress? Certainly not the members of the congregation, for their faces indicated that they were not the least convinced of his wisdom by his attempts at profundity.

A second thing word choice can convey is lack of precision in communication. Words have nuances or shades of meaning. Those nuances are vital to precise communication. If the word that comes to mind for expressing an idea is the first word that comes to mind, but a word that fails to say exactly what you want to say, then find another word. How? Get familiar with a good thesaurus, which is a book of synonyms (words that mean nearly the same things) that spells out the subtle differences between similar-meaning words. A dictionary will give you synonyms, but most dictionaries do not help you know when to use one word in place of another. A thesaurus will do just that.

For example, how do you suppose the apostles of Jesus felt toward Judas after that fatal kiss in the garden of Gethsemane? Words such as *hostility, animosity, rage, bewilderment, anger, abandonment, betrayal* are all appropriate. But each has nuances that make that word mean something slightly different from the rest. A good thesaurus will help spell out those differences so that you can make precisely the point you want to make. I've known preachers whose thesauri were almost as worn as their Bibles.

But don't neglect that dictionary, either. I had to check my dictionary to find the exact plural form of *thesaurus* as I wrote the last sentence of the previous paragraph. A good dictionary will help you avoid mistakes that interfere with careful communication of the gospel. An isolated example: How many times have I heard a preacher say something such as, "Statistical data shows..." Ouch. Statistics is the scientific study of data, so the word *statistical* is unnecessary in that sentence. And the word *data* is the plural form of the word (*datum* is the singular), so the verb in the sentence has to be plural (*show* instead of *shows*). Another way to write that sentence is, "Statistics show..."

Straining at gnats? Not if you want to communicate the gospel effectively.

A word about the use of colloquialisms in a sermon: Don't. A colloquialism is a word or expression that is used in informal conversation. The problem with colloquialisms is that such words or phrases often have a regional or local meaning that does not extend beyond a geographic area. You may think all the members of the congregation to whom you are preaching are familiar with the colloquialisms you want to use, but they are not. Check your sermon for colloquialisms and excise them, get them out of there. I don't care if everyone in the community talks the same way; such speech has no place in the proclamation of the gospel.

Let me give you an example: Many years ago I moved to Tennessee from Massachusetts. On my second or third day in Tennessee, I heard a new friend say he was going to be gone for the afternoon because he had to carry his wife to the doctor. Immediately I wondered under what kind of burden he must be living if his wife was so infirm that he had to take her in his arms, lift her, and transport her by his own strength into the doctor's office. I quickly learned that in that part of Tennessee, the word *carry* was often used as a synonym for the word *take*. My new friend and I chuckled about that many times, but it taught both of us that colloquialisms do not always communicate what we think they do. We cannot assume as we are preaching, especially guest preaching to an unfamiliar congregation, that all of our hearers are familiar with the regional patterns of speech in our area.

Words have power, so choose and use them wisely and carefully. If you are the least bit uncertain about your choice of a word, look it up. The dictionary and thesaurus must become good friends and trusted guides for all your sermon writing.

Some Quick Hints on Style

Each of us has her or his own style of writing and speaking, so no one style is right or wrong. But let me list here a few thoughts about style that might help strengthen your sermon:

Use transitive sentences wherever possible. A transitive sentence starts with a noun, uses an action verb, then moves to a direct object. The opposite kind of sentence, an intransitive sentence, uses an intransitive verb; that is, a part of the verb *to be* as its main verb. Example: Intransitive sentences often start with "There is," "There are," or "It is." These can be appropriate grammatically, but they are not interesting to hear. Contrast "There are many promises for us in the Bible" with "The Bible is filled with many promises for us." Catch the difference? The second sentence is more alive than the first sentence.

Use the active voice rather than the passive voice where possible. In the passive voice, the subject is acted on; in the active voice, the subject acts. An example of the passive voice: "The sermon on the Mount was preached by Jesus." The active voice: "Jesus preached the Sermon on the Mount." What's the hint that you're using the passive voice? Some form of the verb *to be* is used with a past participle of the second verb (usually ending in *ed*). The active voice is just more interesting and more engaging than the passive voice. And despite what some people may think, the passive voice does not make you sound more intelligent.

And don't forget the KISS cliché, for it relates to sermon writing as well as to many other things. KISS stands for Keep It Short and Simple. This doesn't mean that the sermon itself has to be short, but write short sentences where possible and use simple sentences, as appropriate, rather than convoluted, complex sentences. Study the words of Jesus, especially contrasted with the words of Paul. Jesus spoke in simple, direct sentences; Paul often wrote flowery and complicated sentences. We cannot mistake the meaning in Jesus' short, direct sentences; we might lose the meaning in some of Paul's sometimes complicated sentences, such as Romans 1:1-7.

Finally...

You're right; writing a sermon is tough going, but the result is worth every bit of effort you put into the sermon. If you're like most new preachers, you'll discover that the process of rewriting, revising, and editing that sermon takes even longer than writing it in the first place. But the great sense of satisfaction in doing your best to proclaim the good news of the gospel in the clearest, most direct manner will more than repay all your effort.

Someone once asked me how long writing a sermon required. I have no standard response to that. However, I would guess that we ought to spend an hour of preparation (study, research, writing, rewriting, checking, and verifying) for every minute we spend preaching that sermon.

Unrealistic? Not if you want to do your best to proclaim the gospel of Jesus Christ.

9

LEAVE 'EM LAUGHING?

The Use—and Misuse—of Humor in the Pulpit

Y ou're right; the question mark at the end of this chapter title gives a hint of what we're going to be discussing, at least at the beginning of this chapter: humor in the pulpit, telling jokes during the sermon. Should you, or shouldn't you?

Let's start out with several observations.

First, a sermon is not an after-dinner speech such as you might hear at a service club. After-dinner speeches often begin with a joke. But the functions and purposes of sermons and after-dinner speeches are completely different, totally at variance one with the other. And the preacher who models his or her sermons after successful after-dinner speakers is going to fail to proclaim the gospel of Jesus Christ and instead entertain (at best).

Second, God does have a sense of humor. We can see it around us on all sides. The old idea that Christians need to be long-faced and serious all the time is nonsense. We have the greatest message in the world, and our task is to proclaim it joyfully, positively, enthusiastically. Many people talk about joy in the Lord, but their faces certainly don't show it. And many people fail to understand much of the subtle humor in the Bible. We sometimes read the Bible so seriously that we miss those moments of laughter and humor in the text.

> One of the things we miss in the Bible, especially in the Old Testament, is the liberal use of puns or plays on words. We miss these, of course, because we don't know biblical Hebrew and because puns don't translate well, if at all, from one language to another. Several Old Testament names, for example, and a number of statements made by Old Testament characters are puzzling to us or just do not convey much meaning. If we understood the nuances of the Hebrew language, we would chuckle, as the ancient Israelites did as they heard these sentences.

Third, few of us tell jokes well. That's why we laugh at professional comedians, those skilled at telling jokes. Sadly, many of us think we're good joke tellers, but even the best of us is only about average. If you and I are honest with ourselves, we'd probably have to admit that more often than not, the jokes we tell fall flat. And a practiced joke almost always falls flat. When we try to repeat a good joke that really made us laugh, we may get some polite laughter; but we seldom get the reaction we had when we heard that joke.

Why? Because the essence of humor is spontaneity. The times you and I have been truly funny is when we've said or done something spontaneous that struck others as humorous.

Given these comments, what is the place of humor in the pulpit? Humor belongs in the pulpit if it is genuine, appropriate, sensitive, and relevant. Humor does not belong in a sermon if its only purpose is to insert humor into the sermon.

A Handful of Guidelines

Let's spell this out with a series of comments on humor in sermons:

- A humorous story or anecdote must be relevant to the point of the sermon and must illuminate and illustrate the sermon's point.
- A humorous story or anecdote is most effective if it is part of the ongoing development of the sermon (remember spontaneity) rather than freestanding or outside the logical, sequential development of the sermon.
- Any humorous story or anecdote must be brief, very brief, to be effective. Again, the so-called one-liners used by skilled comedians make points better than long, drawn-out, detail-filled stories. In fact, a carefully chosen, truly relevant one-liner that fits perfectly into a sermon will do much to get the wandering minds of listeners tuned back to you.

Another reason humor in a sermon must be brief is that humor is never the point of the sermon. I must confess I've heard twenty-minute sermons in which the first ten minutes were devoted to a long, rambling, detailed story or joke that was only marginally connected to the point of the sermon. Long, involved jokes are no more effective than long, involved sermons. Remember the KISS (Keep It Short and Simple) approach from the last chapter? That works for jokes or humorous anecdotes in the pulpit, too. I'd suggest that if you can't tell a humorous story or anecdote in three simple sentences, that story is too long to tell as part of your sermon.

- We can poke fun in a sermon at our natural human foibles, but we cannot, we must not, poke fun at people of any kind.

Under no circumstances can we tell jokes, stories, or anecdotes that make fun, even in the most gentle way, of groups of people. Examples? Never tell jokes or humorous anecdotes about mothers-in-law, spouses, professions (such as doctors, lawyers, farmers, preachers), people of certain ages, people from particular parts of the nation, and so forth. And certainly any jokes, even the slightly humorous anecdotes (no matter how seemingly harmless), about people with exceptionalities, people of particular races or nationalities, or people of particular socioeconomic or cultural backgrounds are absolutely forbidden under any circumstances.

We must never tell jokes, stories, or anecdotes about particular physical characteristics, such as weight, height, the presence or absence of hair, or other conditions over which people have little or no control. (I'm bald and have worn a full beard for more than a quarter century. I used to joke about my baldness and beard until I realized I was joking about others in the congregation as well.)

Please do not make your children the butt of your pulpit stories or jokes. Your children are a gift to you from God; they are not the means for you to appear humorous. To repeat an earlier point, jokes about spouses, especially your spouse, are never appropriate. A joke about your spouse reveals a lack of respect for your spouse, and to do so publicly (that is, from the pulpit) is especially inappropriate. (Yes, I've done it. I've joked about both my children and my spouse. My children and spouse said that they didn't mind, but no one likes to be publicly humiliated; and that's what a joke about your spouse or children does. I was wrong in joking about them.) Joking about one's spouse or children is wrong; it's hurtful; it's insulting. Don't do it. Don't even be tempted to do it just once because it's a cute little story.

When Can You Tell a Joke?

You may be thinking, *What is there left about which to joke?* Good question. If your answer is *not much,* you're fairly on target. Few things are appropriate for jokes from the pulpit. Rather than tell an inappropriate anecdote or joke, leave them for other settings. Relating a humorous incident once in a great while is much more effective than using humor in some way in every sermon.

What I'm describing here is not a pattern for long-faced, dull sermons. The gospel is good news, and we need to tell it joyfully, delightedly, happily. We need to let our faces, our words, and our actions in the pulpit convey the joy we feel in all that God has done for us. Our sermons and our deportment must reflect the thankfulness we genuinely feel. Study the great preachers; they all preached with a smile on their faces and with a thankful, joyful lilt in their voices. Everything about them conveyed their faith that, no matter what, God was still in control. Great preachers do not make other people the butt of their jokes in order to appear clever or humorous.

Preacher Stories

Years ago, an earnest young man came up to me after a service of worship in the small-membership church I was serving. He said, "Let me ask you a question. Those stories that you tell to illustrate your sermons—are they true, or do you dress them up a little to make your point?" I thought long and hard before I answered. Then I gave him the best answer I could: "Yes."

Since preaching began—and that was long before Jesus walked on earth—preachers have told stories. Stories illustrate ideas, make points, and leave listeners with something to remember. Stories humanize abstract ideas and emphasize basic truths in ways few other devices can.

The Old Testament has its stories told by preachers and prophets. Remember the trees choosing a king in Judges 9:7-15? Or the story Nathan told when he sought to convict David of David's sinfulness (2 Samuel 12:1-4)? Did the trees actually have this conversation? I doubt it. Did Nathan know of a specific person who had been treated as the man with the ewe lamb had in the story he told David? Probably not.

So, must the stories be true? The question is almost irrelevant. Did Jesus know of a particular person when he told the story of the good Samaritan (Luke 10:30-37)? Did he have specific people in mind when he described the father with the two sons or the woman who lost a coin (Luke 15)? Was he personally acquainted with the laborers in the vineyard who thought they had been victims of unfair treatment in that puzzling story in Matthew 20:1-16?

In every case, the point of the story is not the story itself but the message that can be derived from the story. Jesus cared little if his listeners forgot the details of the story of the nobleman and the ten pounds in Luke 19:12-27 ("Did the first servant receive one pound, and did the second servant receive five pounds or three pounds?"), but Jesus certainly wanted them to remember that diligence is rewarded; sloth is not.

Can we, as twenty-first-century preachers, tell stories in our sermons? Can we make up stories to emphasize our points, as Jesus and others apparently did?

A couple of quick responses to those questions:

First, we need to recognize that all the stories that Jesus told were real, believable, and genuine; therefore, they did not have to be literally true. No one would have trouble imagining a shepherd so concerned about one lost sheep that he wandered the hillsides looking for it, or picturing a sower scattering seed and noting that some fell among thorns, some in shallow ground, and some on good, lush soil. A key to the success of the stories or parables told by Jesus (and by successful preachers since the time of Christ) is that the stories are real, believable, familiar, and grounded in everyday life and situations that all can understand. Without any evidence to support this, I would guess that every one of the stories or parables Jesus told had its basis in an experience or situation with which Jesus was familiar. Now, Jesus may have embellished the details just a bit to make his point. However, his point was never in the details; it was in the whole of the story.

Second—and I may tread on some sensitive toes here—I doubt that any of us can develop stories as effectively as Jesus developed stories, and I'm certain that none of us can tell stories as effectively as Jesus told them.

> For instance, notice the incredible economy of words in Jesus' parables. Jesus said more by what he didn't say than by what he did. He didn't have to tell us that the man beaten by thieves and left half dead by the roadside was terrified, then hopeful when he saw the priest approaching, then even more devastated when the priest walked by on the other side of the road. Jesus doesn't bother to tell us how the father of the one we know as the prodigal son felt after his son left home. He leaves that to us to feel and to experience.

If we can't develop and tell stories like Jesus did, what do we do? Here are two possibilities:

- Rely on the stories Jesus told. Use them over and over again. You and I can't tell the stories Jesus told too often. His parables are as new today as they were in that day. Oh, we may have to paraphrase just a bit, because few people of our time know much about being a shepherd, for example, but the stories are still vital. A couple of our great hymns emphasize this point. Remember "I love to tell the story, for those who know it best seem hungering and thirsting to hear it like the rest" or "Tell me the stories of Jesus I love to hear" (*The United Methodist Hymnal*, 156 and 277)?

- And the second possibility is to rely on some of the other great storytellers of an earlier time and of our time. Classical literature of all ages and all cultures is filled with great stories that make significant points. The history of humankind is filled with stories that illustrate almost every conceivable dimension of life. Children's literature and materials (*Aesop's Fables*, C.S. Lewis, and a multitude of other writers) provide an unending source of illustrations, anecdotes, and ideas and stories that fit precisely what we want to say in our sermons. (Even popular culture—that is, television programs and motion pictures—occasionally include elements that can illustrate sermons if these elements are chosen carefully. Always be clear, directly or indirectly, that using an element from a television program or a motion picture is not necessarily an endorsement of that program or movie.)

You may be thinking, *How do I find good illustrative material in classical and contemporary literature? Are indices of these kinds of things available?*

An answer to the second question first: No, I know of no good indices of illustrative material from classical literature or contemporary literature. And please stay away from speaker's books that offer "1,000 illustrations for speeches" or "hundreds of snappy anecdotes to spice up your after-dinner talks."

What preachers must be, need to be, is well read. We need to spend our time reading widely in the great literature of all cultures, in the history of our world, our nation, our communities. We need to plumb the depths of good fiction, serious history, great poetry. We need to be involved in lifelong learning that equips us ever more to preach effectively.

When we use a story or illustration from any source, we need to be careful to give credit to that source in the sermon. This credit can be a couple of words; it need not be a formal citation such as we would use for a term paper. It's both embarrassing and credibility-shaking for a preacher to tell a story or use an illustration as if it were his or her own and then hear a member of the congregation remark that he or she had read that same story in a magazine just last week. I know, for it's happened to me. Ouch!

You've heard great preachers tell stories, and perhaps you've wondered to yourself how they always seem to have exactly the right illustrations for every point. Great preachers get those illustrations not from some master lists of sermon illustrations but from their own reading and study; their own careful immersion in literature, history, and other disciplines; and their own observations of the world in which they live. Great preachers are avid readers, who read broadly and widely. Great preachers are thinking of the proclamation of the gospel of Jesus Christ as they read. Great preachers jot down stories and illustrations that strike them, for they know that those same illustrations and stories will strike others. Great preachers are great students, great learners.

How do you find time for this? You're probably already working a full-time job; you're probably a family member with responsibilities; you're devoting twenty hours a week to detailed sermon preparation using commentaries, dictionaries, concordances, and atlases. How do you find time?

You don't find time. You make time.

Preaching the gospel of Jesus Christ is serious business, for you are dealing with the eternal souls of the people you preach to. Preaching the gospel of Jesus Christ demands your best, and it is rigorous, challenging, difficult. It demands a level of self-discipline of which you may not have known you were capable. God has called you for this task, and God will enable you to fulfill it.

An Addendum

As long as we're talking about jokes and stories told in the pulpit, let me add a comment about another phenomenon I've witnessed several times lately. I don't know if this is a trend or a series of coincidences, but I've heard several preachers in the last year or so break out into song as part of their sermons. They have sung a hymn or a verse from a hymn, always unaccompanied, and the hymns or the verses they have chosen have illustrated their sermons well.

Unless you are a trained and accomplished vocalist, please leave this to others. To sing an unaccompanied solo as part of the sermon is a bit pretentious. And if the text of a hymn or verse of a hymn really illuminates your sermon, then read or recite that text as poetry. Your listeners will hear those words in new ways, and the impact will be multiplied.

10

GET SET

Practice, Rehearsal, and Tryout

Congratulations. You've written a manuscript of your sermon; and although it took several edits and re-edits, you're satisfied with it. Perhaps you even had to start over several times. If so, welcome to the club. Every preacher has had that experience. And many great preachers will tell you that they often go way back to the beginning, to the point of reidentifying and redefining that main point, because their original point simply did not develop adequately. Never be afraid to start over, and over and over.

You've checked out the grammar carefully. (That's crucial.) You've verified the pronunciation of several words of which you were unsure. And you've changed a few words to make the manuscript easier for people to understand. No sermon is improved by using complex and unusual words where simple words will do. If you're anything like I am, you have a mental list of words with which you're just not comfortable. (For example, I am never sure of the pronunciation or meaning of the word *hubris*. It's a good English word, but since I am not comfortable using it, I don't. And I must confess that I have never mastered to my satisfaction the past tenses and past participles of the verbs *lie* and *lay*. Because I want to be as sure of my meanings as possible when I preach, I often substitute another word for these troublesome conjugations.)

You've also checked and rechecked your illustrative material to be sure it makes the points you want to make. You have thrown out any illustrations or stories that were there simply because they're neat stories. If they did not strengthen the communication of the point or subpoint you want to make, you rejected and replaced or omitted a story in that spot altogether.

And you've looked at your use of humor. What humor you've written into your sermon is gentle, simple, and brief. Most important of all, it is totally nonoffensive, even to the most hypersensitive person you can imagine. Again, better no humor than risk humor that some could interpret, even indirectly, as a putdown, an insult, or an example of stereotyping.

You or We?

Now go back and read that manuscript critically one more time. This time focus on the people in the congregation to whom you will be preaching.

Watch your use of pronouns (those generic little words that stand for names). In most sermons, the pronouns *I* and *me* should be used sparingly. The pronoun *you* should seldom be used. The pronouns *we* and *us* should be used much more frequently.

Why? Because a preacher is talking to her or himself as she or he talks to the congregation. Many great preachers and teachers of preaching have said that the best sermons are those in which the preacher talks to her or himself and allows the congregation to listen.

Except in the case of the rare, extremely prophetic sermon, you are not lecturing the congregation on what *they* should be doing or thinking. Instead, you are describing what *we*, as God's people, should be doing and thinking. That's right: You, as the preacher, and the listeners who are in the congregation make up the community of faith; and, as the old saying goes, "You're all in this together." A preacher broadcasts arrogance in telling people how *they* should live; a preacher proclaims togetherness in Christian humility when describing what the gospel calls *us* to be and do.

One More Check

Here's another neat little exercise to help you critique your manuscript. Put all your papers, documents, drafts, and everything else aside. Now, read the manuscript. Then write an outline of the manuscript. You remember what an outline is: points, subpoints, perhaps sub-subpoints, in a logical, developing sequence.

Could you write an outline of that manuscript from this reading? Good.

Now, compare this outline with the outline of the sermon you prepared early in the process, the outline you developed before you began to write the manuscript. It's there in that pile of notes and papers.

The *before* outline and the *after* outline should be similar. If not, then where's the problem, and what happened? (I'm not suggesting that the outlines have to match up perfectly in subpoint after subpoint. But the general shape and flow of the outlines should be similar.) This check will help you determine if you have really focused on that single main point you want to make in the sermon. Straying off to other issues or subsidiary points is always easy; many call that chasing rabbits. And chasing rabbits can take over a sermon if we're not careful. So, take a minute to do this outline exercise. With every sermon, every time? Maybe not. But if you're a beginning preacher, you'll find that this keeps you on the track you set for yourself in this message.

Now What?

OK. You've completed all the checks. The sermon manuscript is there on your desk. You feel good about it. It's ready to go, but you're not quite ready to go yet. So, what do you do?

Remember the silly joke about the stranger in New York City who asked the resident of the city how to get to Carnegie Hall? The resident replied, "Practice, man, practice." We could paraphrase that with, "How do we get from the sermon in manuscript form to a sermon delivered before a congregation." Part of the answer is, "Practice."

Your first step in practicing, in getting ready, is reading your entire manuscript aloud. You don't need an audience yet, not even your spouse. Read it aloud in a normal speaking tone and do a couple simple things as you read it aloud.

First, of course, you must time your sermon. No, you don't need a stop watch or anything like that. But get an idea of how much time is required to read the sermon at a normal speaking pace. Keep in mind that the time required to *preach* the sermon may be only a close approximation to the reading aloud time. Does preaching take more time or less time? That's up to you. But preaching a manuscript often takes more time than reading a manuscript aloud. A ballpark estimate is that preaching the manuscript will take about ten to fifteen percent more time than reading it aloud. Thus, a manuscript that *reads* in fifteen minutes would take about seventeen or so minutes to *preach*. We'll get into why in a later chapter.

Second, read your sermon aloud to catch any strange combinations of syllables that could be trouble when preached. Words put together for reading silently can sometimes trip us up badly when read aloud. So, this reading is in some ways like another edit to be sure you don't have any of those bothersome strings of sounds. "Saul simply sought Samuel" is a satisfactory and correct English sentence that gives no trouble when read silently. But read it aloud, and you'll discover your tongue doing backflips in your mouth. You might want to change the wording to something such as, "Saul was looking for Samuel." This revised sentence is much easier to say.

Don't be afraid to edit and re-edit the manuscript. You want your sermon to be the best it can be and to communicate the gospel as clearly and as directly as possible.

Here's a possible next step in practicing that sermon: Read the sermon aloud again. This time, try looking up from the manuscript several times. But read aloud the first two pages only. Now put the manuscript down and think hard: What is the next subpoint you make? Where does the sermon go after these first two pages? If you can't answer that question easily, read the manuscript through several more times.

Read the sermon aloud again while looking up several times, but stop after four pages and recall where the sermon goes on pages five and six. Do the same thing after six pages. Get the idea? You're reading the sermon aloud for practice, but you're also fixing the content and the sequence of the sermon firmly in mind.

Let me give you a quick analogy: Has someone telling you a joke gotten to the point just before the punch line and then said, "Oh, I forgot to tell you back at the beginning that this was a shaggy, long-haired dog." Ruins the whole joke, doesn't it? That's exactly what happens if the development of your sermon gets out of order. So, the practice of reading aloud a couple of pages and then thinking of what comes next serves to help fix that sequence of ideas, the development of your point, in your head.

Just two weeks ago, the lectionary Gospel text was John, chapter nine, the man born blind and the questions the apostles raised about the man's condition. I did not have my sequence firmly fixed in mind at the first of our two worship services, and I introduced the idea contained in John 9:3b before I had said all I had planned to say about verses 2-3a. I found myself stumbling and saying something such as, "We'll get back to this in a moment." Believe me, by the second service that morning, I had that sequence of development clearly in mind, and the whole sermon flowed much more effectively. The sequential development of an idea is extremely important.

Yes, I know some clever preachers do some amazing things with sequence, including flashbacks and other rhetorical techniques. But until you've accumulated years of preaching experience, leave those gimmicks to the experts. Your people will appreciate a direct, logically sequential, clearly developed sermon.

Are you ready to try the sermon on a live listener? Now's the time. Find some-one to listen who can be honest, objective, and detailed. Comments such as, "Great sermon" or, "I didn't get much out of it" are not of any value in reworking your sermon. What you need are details such as, "I couldn't really follow the transition from talking about Solomon to talking about Jesus at about two thirds of the way through the sermon. What was the connection there?" Or, "The story you told about the businessman and the retired banker was a neat little story, but I don't see how it illustrated the point you were trying to make."

Maybe your spouse can be that honest, detailed, objective listener. Maybe you need to recruit a friend. But regardless of whom you invite to listen, ask the per-son to give you full attention and not to listen while doing something else. Listening while washing dishes or folding clothes or, even worse, watching televi-sion is not at all helpful for you. This need for full attention means you may have to arrange a time in advance for this tryout.

After you've read your manuscript for your listener, listen carefully to all the comments. Don't be defensive. Don't come back at constructive criticisms by saying things such as, "What I was trying to say there was…" You won't have a chance to clarify your ideas in the pulpit on Sunday; your sentences must be crystal clear at the outset.

Should you read your sermon for more than one listener? You be the judge of that. If you really think your listener missed some points that you are sure are clear, try the sermon on another listener. Same reaction? Work on the sermon some more. Positive reaction to those sticky points? OK; go with it.

Some Additional Practice Techniques

While nothing replaces a live listener as a way of critiquing your sermon, don't hesitate to use some of the new media if you have easy access to it.

Read your sermon into a tape recorder; then listen to that sermon of yours crit-ically as you play the tape back. A word of warning: Your voice will sound strange to you on even the best of tape recorders. But in many ways that's good, for it forces you to hear that sermon as others might hear it. Listening to a recording of that sermon also helps you identify portions of the sermon where you are speaking too quickly to be understood, points in the sermon where you need more verbal emphasis, and places in the sermon where the development is hard to follow.

What about videotaping your sermon? Sure. I've always been thankful that I studied preaching in seminary before the advent of closed-circuit television or videotape. I never had the humbling experience of watching myself preach during my first couple years of preaching. In fact, the first time I saw myself preach was when our church was invited to present a Sunday worship service over a local television channel. I worked and worked on that sermon and practiced and practiced those gestures, vocal inflections, and all the rest. But I was less than impressed with what I saw, and I was even further humbled when a well-meaning church member said, "That's the way you always look and sound."

If you videotape your sermon and study what you see, be prepared for some surprises. We don't look and sound on video the way we think we look and sound. Furthermore, the video camera tends to exaggerate our shortcomings. But videotaping can still be a useful tool in practicing that sermon.

On-Site Practice

Another practice technique is on-site practice, if this is possible and convenient. On-site practice is just what the words imply: practicing your sermon in the church where you will be preaching it. You'll get a feel for the pulpit, for the space behind and around the pulpit, and the other characteristics of the space in which you'll be preaching.

I was asked to preach at a rural church several years ago as a last-minute fill-in for a pastor who had become ill. I'd never been in the church before the Sunday I arrived to preach. So, I was somewhat taken aback by the fact that the ceiling and the roof of the church were supported by large pillars in the center of the nave and that one of these pillars was squarely in front of the pulpit and only about eight feet from the pulpit. I got through the sermon all right, but if I'd seen that space before I preached, I would have made some adjustments in the way I stood and moved as I preached.

On-site practice can be daunting from another standpoint. Early in my preaching experience—perhaps it was the second or third sermon I preached—I was asked to preach in a church about a hundred miles away. I wanted to fill the pulpit and do a good job, so I asked a pastor friend if I could practice my sermon in his church a few days before I was to preach. He readily agreed but warned me that the only time that would be available was rather late at night and that he would give me a key to let myself in and out. I jumped at the chance and headed for that old building about ten one evening. I found the lights and went to the pulpit and started my sermon. Because I was alone in a large, old church building, I heard every creak and groan in that structure and was convinced at least half a dozen times that someone else was in the church besides me. Concentrating on my sermon was problematic, to say the least. A moral to this vignette: Try on-site preaching in the daytime, if possible, and take along a listener or two to make things feel more comfortable.

Some Final Thoughts About Practice

Almost as a way of a summary, let me make two quick points to conclude this chapter:

First, nothing in this chapter should be taken to suggest memorizing your manuscript. Yes, you read it over and over again, but please do not memorize your manuscript and preach a memorized sermon. Here are a couple of reasons why I make this point: Few of us are accustomed to memorizing long pieces of prose; some of us haven't memorized anything since our school days. Memorizing long passages of prose takes practice, time, more practice, and more time.

Then, too, if you have memorized your sermon and forget a single line, phrase, or word during the preaching of the sermon, you may lose the direction of the entire sermon. The apparent anxiety, the stumbling, the vocalized pauses (uh, duh, duh-uh, and so forth) are deadly.

Memorizing a sermon gives it a canned, stilted, prepackaged feel. A memorized sermon can sound like fast food for the ear: It may have some nourishment to it, but the joy of eating it is absent.

This brings up the second point I want to make about practice. Practice is essential, but overpractice can destroy a great sermon. I have left many great sermon points in the car, preaching those same points over and over again to myself until they became like rote. With too much practice, we lose the edge, the spontaneity, the passion that should be in a sermon. An overpracticed sermon is like an overcooked meal: the flavor is missing.

Don't use these comments about overpractice as an excuse to avoid practice or to practice just a little. Instead, practice, practice, practice until you feel confident about your sermon but not bored with it. Bored? Yes, bored with the sermon because you have lived with it for so long that it no longer has an edge. Practice reading and rereading the sermon while it still has an exciting freshness for you. When it begins to become routine and stale feeling, stop practicing—and start praying.

Now you're ready to preach.

11
Go!

Delivering the Sermon

The day has almost arrived for that first sermon. You think you have your sermon well in hand; you feel good about it because you've worked long and hard on it and surrounded your work with prayer. But a couple of details remain.

What Do I Take to the Pulpit?

Soon after you think your sermon is ready, you'll have to decide what to take to the pulpit. Put simply, you have several choices:

- You could take the entire manuscript.
- You could take an outline.
- You could take note cards.
- You could take two or all of these.

Take the Entire Manuscript?

Many beginning preachers always take their sermon manuscript with them into the pulpit and preach from the manuscript. This is a fairly solid approach. After all, you have labored on that manuscript; you have lived with it; you have read and reread it many times by now. You know that manuscript.

Preaching from a manuscript does not mean standing in the pulpit reading the manuscript. That is deadly. However, it can mean using the manuscript as a constant point of reference to which you can glance repeatedly to be sure you are making your points in sequence and in good order.

If you plan to preach from your manuscript (and I'd suggest you do so the first couple of sermons), you might want to

- enlarge the type size on your manuscript, perhaps two or three sizes, to make the type easier to see at a glance. Also, if you haven't done this already, double or even triple space your manuscript. These adjustments to your manuscript are easy to do with a computer word-processing program.

- widen the margins on each side of the page so that you can write in notes and reminders to yourself within the manuscript. Don't put these notes in the body of the manuscript; you'll never find them. What kinds of notes? Reminders about gestures, voice inflections, posture, and so forth.

- number your manuscript pages boldly. Put big numbers in an obvious place, perhaps the top right corner of each page. Nothing is more frustrating than turning two pages instead of one and totally losing your place.

- print your manuscript on one side of the paper only. You should never have to pick up your manuscript or a page of your manuscript (unless, of course, you are reading a direct quotation from a source). You may want to turn the corner of the pages just a little so that you can easily slide the top page off the remaining pages as you go through the sermon.

What About Using an Outline?

Fine, if you're comfortable with outlines. The first several times you preach with an outline, err on the side of too much detail in the outline. I remember once seeing a sermon outline that consisted of five words. But that was an outline by an experienced preacher, a preacher who had devoted hours and hours of study and preparation and manuscript writing and rewriting into those five words. Unless you have that much experience preaching under your belt, leave the single-word outlines to others.

As with the manuscript, print your outline in a large, strong typeface that you can read easily at a glance. Don't be afraid to double or triple space your outline, and, again, number those pages boldly and clearly.

Take Note Cards?

Some effective preachers use three-by-five or four-by-six note cards in the pulpit. In many cases, these note cards constitute an outline of the sermon, but usually each note card contains only one point and its subpoints. Even though your sermon may have one central focus or point, you may need five to six steps or points to make that central point. A preacher using note cards would have each of those five or six steps on a separate note card, with prominent card numbers. I've tried the note cards and often use them when leading workshops, but I seem to be able to handle sheets of paper more easily in the pulpit than I handle note cards.

The choice is up to you, but my suggestion is that you use the manuscript the first several times you preach. Get a little experience and confidence; then try the outline and the note cards. (I must confess that when I preached my first sermon, I took my handwritten manuscript, a typed manuscript, an outline, and a stack of note cards into the pulpit. I wasn't leaving anything to chance. Fortunately, I could put everything but the typed manuscript on a small shelf under the pulpit, and I preached from the manuscript. Knowing that all the other stuff was there gave me a sense of security.)

You have your manuscript ready and your Bible marked with the passages you're going to read as part of your sermon. You've prayed and prayed about this sermon since the invitation to preach came your way. You feel good about your preparation. It's Saturday; tomorrow is the day.

Pulpit Attire

One thing that confuses many beginning preachers is what to wear to preach. Sounds insignificant, but it can be an issue.

First, remember the symbolism of the preaching robe worn by clergy. Traditionally, the preaching robe hides the personality of the preacher so that the message of the gospel can come through. A robe was intended to eliminate the listeners' distractions; that is, a robe was to help the listeners focus on the message and not on the person who was delivering the message. Although you, as a lay speaker, will not be wearing a robe, the same principle applies: Do not call attention to yourself by your attire.

The most appropriate attire for men is a dark suit, a solid color (preferably white) shirt, and a conservative necktie. Leave the flashy sports jackets and the loud neckties for other occasions. Do not wear white socks, for they scream as you walk across the chancel.

The most appropriate attire for women is a dark dress or business suit with modest and conservative lines. Avoid flowing scarves, unusually high heels, and daring color combinations.

Women and men should go easy on the jewelry, especially the heavy neck chains (even if they hold a cross), large metallic bracelets, and dangling earrings.

Are you getting the idea? Anything that distracts the listeners' attention from your message should be eliminated.

> Sometimes family members want to purchase a preaching robe for a beginning ordained preacher. This is a nice gesture of confidence. If your family wants to buy you a robe, encourage them to purchase a plain black robe or a natural color alb. Leave the unusual colors, the satin panels, the embroidered symbols, the stripes on the sleeves, and all the other accouterments for others. Remember, the robe is intended in part to hide the person of the preacher behind the message of the gospel, not to draw attention to itself.

While You're Waiting

You've arrived at the church; you've met the lay leader and the person who will serve as liturgist. You've gone over the order of worship again and know that you are responsible for the Scripture just before your sermon and for the sermon itself. The liturgist has pointed out where you are to sit during the service. This is most often on the chancel (the raised area up front where the pulpit and altar are located) or occasionally in a front pew. The liturgist has also given you instructions on coming to the chancel. Perhaps you will process behind the choir; perhaps you and the liturgist will come to the chancel together from a side door; perhaps you and the liturgist will simply go up to the chancel following the announcements or when the prelude begins.

But please remember that although you are the preacher this morning, you are also a full participant with this community of believers in a service of worship. And remember that since you are probably unknown to many in this congregation, people may be glancing at you from time to time. So, stand and sing (modestly) when the congregation stands and sings, pray with the congregation, take part fully in this service of worship.

A couple of little things: While sitting on the chancel waiting for the sermon time, be careful about your deportment. Yawning, nose-blowing, excessive scratching, and constant wiggling are of course *out*. Careful attention to what is being said and done by the liturgist is *in*.

It's Your Turn

Suddenly, the congregation has reached the time in the service of worship for your Scripture reading and the sermon. (I hope you've asked the liturgist or lay leader to avoid a long, flowery introduction of you.)

You walk confidently to the pulpit and you're ready to go. First, take a deep breath and look around at the congregation. Try to see everyone in the congregation. A little smile on your face will go a long way to put you and your listeners at ease. Take another deep breath. Your mouth is going to feel dry, and you're gong to be anxious. A couple of deep breaths will help a lot.

Hold your Bible in your hand; don't leave it on the pulpit as you read from it. People won't be able to hear you with your head buried in the Bible on the pulpit. Remind the congregation of the source of the reading: "Today's Scripture lesson is from Paul's letter to Rome, chapter 8, verses 5 through 11." Give people a moment to find that passage in their Bibles. Feel free to provide a little bit of background. For example, if you are reading a passage from Ezekiel, you might say, "Ezekiel wrote these words in exile in Babylon with those who have been deported from Jerusalem." Go ahead and use names in place of pronouns in the biblical text if it will assist your listeners. Many Gospel passages start with "And he went from there..." Reading that text as "And Jesus went from there . . ." is perfectly appropriate. Use the congregation's tradition to end the Scripture reading, perhaps saying something such as, "The Word of God for the people of God." If it is the congregation's tradition, they will respond with "Thanks be to God!"

Invite the congregation to join you in a short prayer before the sermon. Some preachers use, "Let the words of my mouth and the meditations of our hearts be acceptable in your sight, O Lord" (adapted from Psalm 19:14) or a similar kind of prayer. Most preachers follow this prayer with a moment of silent prayer, take another deep breath, and then begin. Proclaim the good news of Jesus Christ, as you have prayerfully and diligently prepared that sermon.

Posture and Gestures

What do you do with your hands once you've begun? First, please forget the tripod. What's the tripod? That is the tendency we all have to place our hands, arms outstretched, on the sides of the pulpit—and leave them there. From the perspective of the congregation, it looks as if we're hanging on for dear life (perhaps we are). But that tripod can become rigid and fixed and completely detract from the message you're delivering.

Second, your hands do not belong in your pockets while you are preaching. Yes, I know many men have a habit of putting their hands in their pockets as they speak, but resist this temptation. I once threatened to sew up the pockets on my trousers to keep me from doing this

Third, try to avoid prolonged periods with your hands clasped in front of you, like a classical singer.

All of these postures can be distracting and artificial. Instead, use your hands as you use them in everyday conversation. Let the gestures flow from the content and context of your sermon. Practiced, studied gestures can appear phony. Instead, get so caught up in the message you are proclaiming that the gestures flow naturally.

Does this mean that you are to wander all over the chancel? Of course not, for wandering is distracting. But it does suggest that you can move from side to side and from back to front as the content of the sermon moves you. If you are preaching from your manuscript, and if your manuscript is double or triple spaced and printed in a good sized type, you can move about without losing your place. Standing firmly rooted in place as if your shoes are bolted to the floor can detract as much from your message as wandering aimlessly all over the chancel.

Where Do You Look?

Eye contact with the members of the congregation is vital to an effective sermon. Look around the entire nave (the area in front of the chancel, where the congregation is seated) as you preach. If the choir is behind you, turn and look at the choir members from time to time. Forget the old clichés about public speaking. Picking out one person in a back row and preaching to that one person is not an effective means of focusing. And please forget that trite saying about imagining your congregation in pajamas or underwear. This is utterly demeaning, disrespectful, and totally ineffective.

Where *do* you look? You are talking with a group of friends. Look at them as you talk with them, just as you look at people with whom you are talking in other situations. Some teachers of public speaking recommend sweeping the audience with the eyes on a regular, rhythmic basis. This can become so programmed, so conscious, that it becomes and appears artificial and forced. Simply look at your friends as you are sharing the gospel with them.

Obviously, you are not going to stare at the unruly child or the crying baby; neither are you going to stare at the gentleman who is snoring gently or the teenagers who are whispering. All of these will likely be in the congregation to whom you are preaching, but you are preaching to the whole congregation, not just to the handful who seem not to be listening carefully.

You are going to be looking down at your manuscript from time to time, but don't become so buried in that manuscript that you don't look at your listeners. (And don't look at your listeners so much that you neglect the manuscript.)

Beware of the Monotone

I suggested in an earlier paragraph that the content and context of the sermon should help dictate gestures and movement in the pulpit. Exactly the same can be said for vocal inflection and the use of pauses in the sermon.

Few things are more difficult to hear than a monotone voice; that is, a speech or sermon delivered at one level pitch of voice throughout. If you are passionate about the content of your sermon—if you are not, you ought not to be preaching it—your voice is going to rise and fall naturally to emphasize the points you are trying to make. Just as studied, artificial gestures are ineffective, so are studied, artificial changes in vocal inflection. These changes in your voice ought to be as natural as the changes in vocal inflection when you are talking with a friend about something that interests you both greatly.

Listen as others speak to you and as you speak to others. Sometimes the speech is slow and deliberate, sometimes rapid, depending on what is being said. Sometimes the speech is soft and quiet, sometimes loud and emphatic, again depending on what is being said. Let the content of the sermon carry your voice; be passionate about what you are proclaiming; and allow your voice to go in its natural directions. Undue concern with inflection and emphases, especially by a beginning preacher, dooms a sermon. Trust yourself and trust God's guidance as you preach. Make the message come alive.

In using your voice, avoid

- shouting or straining your voice as you preach;
- whispering in the pulpit, for it serves no purpose;
- imitating accents, because to do so is stereotyping people and insulting them;
- speaking with overly dramatic shifts in volume or inflection;
- using a voice other than your own, such as a falsetto or a growl.

Your voice is the tool God gave you to proclaim the gospel, so use it naturally and carefully to God's glory.

A Word About Microphones

You may discover when you arrive at the church that the pulpit is miked; that is, the church uses a sound amplification system to enable people to hear better. If the preachers in that church customarily use the microphone, you will probably be expected to do so also. Essentially, three different kinds of microphones are used in churches, and you may run into one or more of them.

- By far the easiest microphone to use (because you tend to forget about it) is a wireless lapel microphone. Simply fasten the tiny microphone to your garment about six to eight inches below your chin, and put the deck-of-cards-sized box in your pocket or clip it on your belt. Remember to turn the microphone on when you begin, and then forget about it. Don't begin the sermon by asking, "Can you hear me back there?" Congregations that are accustomed to using microphones have people staffing the sound boards who will make you audible.

- A second kind of microphone is the hand-held, usually wired, microphone. This is on a stand on or near the pulpit, and you simply lift it out of the stand if you wish when you begin preaching. Make sure the switch on the handle is on, and speak into it from a distance of about six to eight inches. Feel free to shift hands holding the microphone, and be somewhat aware of the cord so that you don't become wrapped up in it. Remember to hold the microphone six to eight inches from your lips at all times. I've seen preachers speak and gesture with both arms over their heads as they held a microphone. Obviously, a microphone held overhead does no good at all.

- Perhaps the most inconvenient type of microphone is the mike that is permanently attached to the pulpit. The problem here is that you must remember to speak into the microphone, again from six to eight inches away. And since the microphone is fixed, your head must be relatively fixed also.

Using these latter two types of microphones takes practice and experience. If you find such a microphone where you are to preach, take a third and fourth deep breath, and then go preach.

12

NOW WHAT?

Silent Prayer Time, Altar Calls, Transitioning

You're nearing the end of your sermon and are about ready to slide the next-to-the-last page of manuscript over and start on the last page. You feel good about how the sermon has been presented. You found that your gestures were natural; you were surprised at how you modulated your voice; and you discovered that you paused several times during the sermon to let a point connect with your listeners. The people in the congregation have been attentive, and you even saw several heads nodding in agreement and approval of what you've been saying.

Even more significantly, you've felt the power of the Holy Spirit in the congregation as you preached. You can't help but feel that the Spirit has touched you and made you a better preacher than you thought you would be. You're a little confused about time, but that's natural. You feel like the sermon has gone quickly, but in reality it has taken just about the time you planned.

All the prayer, all the study, all the preparation, all the practice, and, again, all the prayer has paid off. You have proclaimed the good news of the gospel and have lifted up Jesus Christ in a way that has given your listeners a sense of joy and hope and a challenge to greater discipleship.

But now you're nearing the conclusion of the sermon, and a thought hits you: *What do I do at the end of the sermon?*

End the Sermon

One of the hardest things for beginning preachers to do is to conclude a sermon. Sounds simple to end a sermon, but it is not. Even though we have written and rewritten that sermon manuscript over and over, most of us as beginning preachers think our conclusions are weak when we near the end of the sermon. I have talked with countless preachers with all different kinds of experience levels, and almost every one of them has reported that ending a sermon is one of the most difficult parts of preaching.

What many of us are tempted to do as the sermon concludes is to try to summarize the sermon again in the last couple minutes of the sermon time. We want to make sure that our point has been heard, so we try to make it again, and again, and again. We fear that some of the development of the sermon may have been lost, so we ad lib a little more to make sure everyone got it. Our sermon ends, as T. S. Eliot said that the world might end, "Not with a bang but with a whimper" (*The Hollow Men*).

If you're having these feelings as you come to the end of the sermon, you are certainly not alone. In fact, I recall one of the most prominent and well-known preachers in our denomination saying, "I don't ever end a sermon; I just quit talking."

Suggestions for this feeling?

• Trust your manuscript. You labored long and hard on it; you diligently prayed over it and with it. Trust the conclusion you wrote into that manuscript. Go with it. You probably can't come up with anything on the spur of the moment that is any better than the ending with which you struggled as you wrote your manuscript.

• Keep in mind that a sermon can end on a bang even though that bang is gentle and quiet and peaceful. A bang ending for a sermon is not always (or even often) a rousing, shouting, bombastic finish. It can just as well be a calm, quiet challenge to renewed life in the Spirit. It can be a gentle nudge toward repentance. It can be a simple invitation to love as Christ has loved us. A good ending is not always the arms-flying, voice-shouting, pulpit-pounding conclusion we see on television. Those theatrics have no place in the pulpit.

A good ending leaves your listeners knowing that they have heard the good news of the gospel and that they have gained new insight into how to live their lives in response to that gospel. A good ending leaves your listeners with a challenge to live their lives in a more Christ-like way every moment. A good ending lifts, assures, and comforts but at the same time invites, challenges, and shows the way.

Don't try to re-preach your whole sermon in a concluding sentence, and don't give into the temptation to think your manuscript ending is weak and that you must ad lib a stronger ending. Trust yourself and the work you have put into your sermon.

What Comes Next?

That nagging feeling comes as the sermon is winding down: *What do I do right after the sermon?*

You probably discussed this some with the lay leader or liturgist before the service began. But if the lay leader or liturgist was like the great majority of these well-meaning people are, the only answer you received was, "Well, we usually have a hymn (or a prayer, or the offering, or something else) after the sermon, but anything you'd like to do is all right with us."

The ball is right back in your court. What do you do after the sermon?

The Matter of Altar Calls

A tradition in a great many congregations is to have some form of an invitation or altar call at the conclusion of the sermon. While the form and style of this altar call varies somewhat by region of the country, the basic elements are similar.

An altar call or invitation, by whatever name it is called and in whatever form or style it is practiced, is an opportunity for the members of the congregation who choose to do so to respond in some way to the proclamation of the gospel they have just heard. It is a way for people to act on the insights and challenges they have experienced as Christ was lifted up in the message. It is a chance for people in the congregation to participate tangibly and openly in the service of worship. The invitation is part of the people's worship.

This means, of course, that an altar call (or whatever you wish to call it) is not only or just an invitation to members of the congregation to confess their sins and accept Jesus Christ as Lord and Savior. Perhaps on some occasions it *will* be just that. But just as often, this sermon-ending call may be an invitation to some other form of commitment, response, challenge, or participation. Unfortunately (again, perhaps because of the popularity of television preachers), the image many of us have of the invitation at the end of the sermon is limited only and exclusively to confessing sins and accepting Christ as personal Savior.

So, what do you do? If you desire to have some sort of invitation or altar call following your sermon, you shape and form that call to the dimension of the gospel about which you have been preaching. In other words, you make the invitation fit the message. Sometimes, of course, this will be an invitation to repentance and acceptance of Christ. At other times, your message will end with an invitation for worshipers to respond in other ways. Consider the following invitations:

- to make a commitment to share the gospel with at least one friend during the coming week;
- to serve the least, the last, and the lost on a regular basis through the congregation's ministry of mission and social concern;
- to have renewed and regular Bible study and prayer;
- to meet with at least three other church members on a regular basis for prayer and meditation;
- to answer the call to lead or teach in the Sunday school;
- to visit on a regular basis with members of the congregation and community who are unable to be in church worship;
- to pray daily for those for whom no one else is praying;
- to dedicate one's talents, abilities, and opportunities to the service of others in the name of Christ;
- to surrender at least one bad habit, grudge, or animosity to Jesus Christ;
- to renew a lifelong commitment to Jesus Christ as Lord of life.

Get the idea? The content and point of your sermon forms and shapes the dimensions of the invitation you give at the end of the sermon. And such an invitation fits both long-term Christians and those new in the faith.

I have often visited with people who have just experienced strong and powerful sermons. Many times I have heard them say something such as, "I was really moved by that message and wanted to respond in some way. But the preacher invited to the Communion rail only those who wanted to accept Jesus Christ as Lord and Savior and those who wanted to unite with the congregation. I'm already a member of the congregation, and I think I accept Christ's love and repent of my sins every day."

Please don't get the idea that I'm criticizing invitations to accept Christ. Accepting Jesus Christ as Lord and Savior is the most important thing any of us will ever do in our lives. But not every sermon leads to that single conclusion. We often preach to congregations of deeply committed Christians who, as theologian Søren Kierkegaard pointed out, accept Christ daily through prayer and service. Thus, what every preacher needs to offer at the end of a sermon is an inclusive invitation (one that will touch all the people in the congregation), not an exclusive invitation (one that will touch nonbelievers only and exclude from response those who are already striving daily to live with Christ).

Forms of Response to Your Invitation

As the preacher in the service, you should issue the invitation or altar call, for you have proclaimed the good news and issued the challenges within the sermon. This invitation should be simple and direct and should include some form of specific activity on the part of those in the congregation. Just what form that response will take depends in part on the physical structure of the nave and chancel.

- You might invite those who wish to respond to the invitation to come to the Communion rail for silent prayer and meditation as the congregation sings a hymn of commitment.
- If no Communion rail is available, you might ask people to come to the front of the nave and stand in silent prayer as the congregation sings.
- You might ask people to raise their hands as a symbol of their willingness to respond to the invitation.
- Another tangible response is to invite members of the congregation to turn to one another and ask one another for prayer as they seek to live out the challenge the gospel has presented to them.
- Yet another response would be to invite the entire congregation to a time of silent prayer in response to the invitation, the challenge, the opportunity. Make such a prayer time truly silent: no singing, no music, just silence to listen to God.
- Other responses might be to fill out cards and place them in the offering plates, to speak to you following the service of worship about their intentions or to signify in some other way their willingness to accept the invitation you have made.

You see, no single invitation covers all sermons and situations, and no single way or means of responding to the invitation fits every proclamation of the gospel and every setting. If the invitation is specific to the sermon you have just preached, the way of response will present itself easily and naturally. And, as with so many other dimensions of preaching, the more simple way is preferable to the more complicated.

But for a sermon to be complete, for the good news of the gospel to be proclaimed effectively, the sermon must include some time and some means—simple as those means might be—for people to respond. As I said in an earlier chapter, one of the least effective ways for people to worship God is to sit passively as someone talks at them. The proclamation of the gospel demands some form of response for worship to take place. In traditional Protestant worship, the invitation or altar call (or whatever this act might be termed in your area) is the means for doing this.

What If They Come?

I remember the first time I preached a revival sermon. I was preaching in a friend's church and had worked long and hard on the sermon. I thought that the sermon had gone quite well, so I was feeling up as the sermon concluded. But my friend had told me to be sure to offer an invitation—he called it an altar call—because this was a revival and people would expect it.

As I was new to all of this and still lacked confidence, I stammered out an invitation that was in line with my sermon, and the congregation started singing the hymn of commitment.

I still clearly remember the sudden feeling I had as the first notes of that hymn sounded. I found myself hoping that no one would respond to the invitation, that no one would come to the Communion rail, because I simply did not know what I should do if they did. I felt instant regret about this thought, offered a silent prayer of confession, then looked toward the congregation. About five people were kneeling at the rail and about another half dozen were coming down the aisles.

I still didn't know what to do, but I have discovered that I did just the right thing: nothing. I simply let this be a moment between these people and God. I did not try to insert myself into their prayers and thoughts, nor did I assume that I could solve whatever problems they might be bringing to the Communion rail. Somewhat to my surprise, several members of the congregation thanked me later for that private moment they had with God. One even remarked that a revival preacher in years gone by had asked each person who responded to the invitation to tell the congregation why she or he was in need of prayer. Then the revival preacher prayed for (not with) each person. In some settings and situations, this might be appropriate, but not in all circumstances.

I have followed this form and style of invitation throughout my ministry. Quite often, I invite people to come to the Communion rail (if appropriate, given the structure of the chancel) and to pray in silence. Sometimes I indicate that if some would like me to pray with them, they can nod to me or otherwise motion to me, and I will be eager to join them in prayer. But this seldom happens. People appreciate a few moments of silence with God. Many people don't want to tell the preacher—especially a guest preacher—why they are coming to the rail. People want to be assured that their prayers are heard, not because of the intercession of the preacher, but simply because God hears their heartfelt prayers no matter how they are offered.

Thanks be to God!

What If No One Comes?

You've offered a sincere invitation to respond to the gospel of Jesus Christ. You announced the hymn of commitment, and the congregation is beginning the next-to-the-last verse. Still, no one has responded to your invitation. You invited people to come to the Communion rail, but no one has moved.

What do you do?

If you were a manipulative preacher, you would interrupt the singing and reissue the call, probably intensifying the invitation and passionately pleading with people to respond.

But thank God you are not a manipulative preacher. You do not interrupt the singing and coax or cajole people into responding to your invitation. You do not shame people into doing what you want them to do. So, what *do* you do?

Again, the answer is *nothing*. Continue through the final verses of the hymn of commitment, and then sit down.

What does a lack of response to your invitation mean? Once more, the answer is *nothing*. That lack of response doesn't mean that your sermon was poorly constructed or poorly delivered. That lack of response does not mean that the congregation missed the point of your sermon. That lack of response does not mean that the people did not understand your invitation.

Most important, that lack of response does not mean that people in the congregation did not respond in their own ways to the gospel you proclaimed. You will never know how many silent prayers were offered during the singing of that hymn. You will never know how much soul searching transpired as those verses were sung. You will never know the joy that filled some hearts in response to your message of good news. But God knows.

The success or effectiveness of a sermon is never judged by the numbers of people who respond to a specific invitation. Individuals have all kinds of reasons for responding and for not responding to an invitation. Do not judge yourself or your sermon on the basis of what you have prescribed as tangible responses.

Instead, sing that hymn following the sermon with a sense of commitment; then take your seat and offer God a silent prayer of praise and thanksgiving for leading, guiding, directing you through the proclamation of the gospel of Jesus Christ.

Because God did just that.

13

HOW DID IT GO?

Listening, Self-critique, and What to Do With the Manuscript

If you are like many beginning preachers who have just completed one of their first sermons and the invitation that followed it, what happened next in the service of worship is a bit of a blur. Perhaps the congregation joined in a closing hymn; perhaps the congregation had the offering following the sermon; or perhaps the congregation joined in the pastoral prayer and our Lord's Prayer following the sermon. But whatever took place, you may have been less than fully concentrating on what was taking place.

Don't worry about this; it is a natural experience of the first-time preacher. Preaching, proclaiming God's Word, is emotionally draining (if it is not, you are not putting enough into it) and can be physically exhausting also. If you could watch some of the great preachers of our day from behind the pulpit, you'd notice that many of them preach on their tiptoes, literally. They are stretching, striving, to announce the good news in the most effective way possible. It is exhausting, a good kind of exhausting.

As time goes by and you preach more and more often, you'll still find yourself worn out at the end of a sermon; but you'll be able to participate more actively and more, should we say, consciously in the remainder of the liturgy.

But regardless of how you're feeling at the end of the sermon, your deportment following the sermon should be the same as before the message. Participate as fully as possible in the liturgy; be aware that you are still sitting before a congregation; and conduct yourself as a representative of those who proclaim God's Word.

Resist the urge, somewhat common in beginning preachers, to gulp down a large glass of water following your sermon. Yes, I know your mouth will be dry, but an inconspicuous sip of water is more appropriate than emptying the tumbler. The same goes for coughing and throat-clearing. You will want to do these following your sermon, but keep them as low-key and unobtrusive as possible. Never resort to the television evangelist's trick of pulling a large handkerchief out of your pocket and mopping your brow with it as if you had just run a sub-four-minute mile.

One of the most glaring breeches of this etiquette that I've seen lately was a preacher who finished his sermon, pulled a handkerchief from his pocket, and proceeded to clean his eye glasses: putting the lenses near his mouth to fog them up and then polishing the lenses, including checking and rechecking them by holding them at arm's length up to the light. I learned later that this was one of this man's first sermons, and I'm sure his elaborate glasses-cleaning ritual was a nervous reaction of some sort. However, he was still in the chancel and in full view of the entire congregation.

After the Service

The lay leader or liturgist should tell you what to do at the conclusion of the service of worship. Most likely, you will be asked to pronounce the benediction either from the front of the church (the preferred location so that you can face the worshipers) or from the back of the sanctuary, near the exit doors. If you are to give the benediction from the back of the sanctuary, you may be invited to walk with the liturgist to the door during the singing of the last hymn. Watch the liturgist for your cue as to when to leave the chancel. Take your hymnal and continue singing as you recess (the liturgical word that means leaving the chancel and walking through the sanctuary to the exit).

You know what happens next. The members of the congregation file past you, shake your hand, and comment on the sermon. It's an invigorating moment, for most of the comments you receive about your sermon will be positive.

But let me make a couple suggestions for making the most of this time. If the liturgist or lay leader is standing with you and introducing people as they leave, try to use each person's name as you greet her or him. You won't remember the name for long; that's all right. If the liturgist says something such as, "This is Mrs. Smith," a comment from you, such as, "Glad to have you in worship today, Mrs. Smith," indicates that you heard the name and valued it enough to repeat it.

Please be sure to greet the children also. Some youngsters may be reluctant to shake hands, so do not force a handshake on them. In many parts of our country in this day, some youngsters will respond to the open hand and the "give me five" invitation. Even the littlest ones in the congregation I serve enjoy doing this, and it builds a relationship that will last and last. Children are a crucial part of the congregation, so do not neglect them.

Some preachers touch a parishioner's forearm or shoulder in addition to shaking her or his hand. But don't do it, especially if you're guest preaching in a congregation of people you don't know. Why? Some people simply do not like physical contact, especially with a stranger. The overfamiliarity that a hand on the shoulder, the arm, or the back implies makes many people uncomfortable. Resist the urge to be effusive in your greetings, as a simple handshake is appropriate and preferred.

Many people will tell you that they enjoyed your sermon. I've always been uncomfortable with that word *enjoy* when applied to a sermon. I don't know if a sermon is something one should enjoy the way one enjoys a television program or a good novel. But that's what people say, probably because many of them do not know what else to say. So, what's your response? Again, remember the KISS (Keep It Short and Simple) approach we've suggested so often. A sincere "Thank you" is all that's needed. Asking for feedback from members of the congregation on particular points or subpoints of the sermon is never appropriate.

What about the critic? Praise God first, for the presence of a critic means someone listened carefully enough to disagree with something you said and to tell you about it. Never get defensive in the face of the critic. A comment such as, "That's an interesting way to look at that passage" or, "I never considered that angle on this parable" affirms the critic, tells him or her that you respect his or her opinion (even if you think he or she is way off base), and tends to close off further discussion. If the critic wants to discuss the point further, fine. Simply ask him or her to wait until the rest of the congregation has left the building; explain that you'll be eager to discuss the point with him or her then. In other words, don't hold up the congregation by getting into an argument with one critic. No one ever wins such arguments, anyway.

Finally, and perhaps most importantly, don't take the comments you hear from members of the congregation too seriously. Graciously accept all the comments, but don't assume that they are the whole truth. Instead, bear in mind that your sermon was not as good as some people made it out to be and wasn't as bad as the few critics seemed to imply. People have told me that my sermon was the best sermon they've ever heard. I don't believe it. Others have told me that my sermon was the worst, most useless sermon they've ever heard. I don't believe that, either.

Perhaps one of the most memorable comments I heard came from a middle-aged woman who said something such as, "I can't believe that I spent fifteen of the few minutes I have left on this planet listening to such gibberish." My first thought was to ask her what she meant, which would have been inappropriate. My second thought was to ask the liturgist who she was and what her problem was. That also would have been inappropriate. My third thought was to say I hoped she found some way to worship God through other components of the service. I tried that, and it seemed to quiet her down a bit. But I'm still not sure it was the best thing I could have said in that situation.

So, Evaluate

We United Methodists are known for our intense interest in evaluating everything. Sometimes it seems that we evaluate the evaluations of our evaluations. But evaluation is necessary, no matter how much we may make light of the process. Evaluations prevent us from repeating our mistakes, prevent us from assuming that passable is sufficiently good, and goad us into constant improvement.

Evaluate that sermon—honestly, carefully, objectively, in detail. You will learn as much about preaching from your own rigorous evaluation of your sermon as you learned in the preparation of that sermon.

How do you evaluate your sermon? I'd suggest several steps.

The first step is to go home (or go out to Sunday dinner, as often happens with a guest preacher) and forget about the sermon for a moment. If the people you are having dinner with want to discuss the sermon, fine. But try to limit the discussion to the points your meal companions raise, not details you raise. Any statement by you that begins with something such as, "How did you like the point I made about...?" or, "What did you think of the illustration of the...?" is going to render almost useless evaluation. You are putting your meal companions on the spot. It would take a strong, courageous individual to make a negative comment in response to such a question during Sunday dinner.

One preacher I knew always said that silence could often be considered critical if the preacher asked for feedback. If your question, "Did you like the part where I said...?" is met with silence by some of your Sunday dinner friends, you might assume that those who are silent were less than impressed with that part.

Back off detailed evaluation at Sunday dinner. It's too soon, and your captive audience is going to be less than objective.

Late Sunday afternoon or Sunday evening is the time for you to do some serious evaluation of the sermon. And the best way to do that evaluation is to do your own evaluation first and then to seek input from others.

Read the manuscript slowly and carefully. Develop a quick code for evaluating how sentences, illustrations, and points were received. I often use different color highlighters. A green highlighter suggests that the sermon moved well at this point or that the illustration seemed to work with this congregation. A red highlighter generally suggests exactly the opposite: This statement didn't work; this illustration fell flat; this point didn't get across the way I expected. I've used a variety of other color highlighters to denote other details of my evaluation, but you'll develop your own system of making notes about how your sermon was received.

But don't be satisfied with just saying, "This went well" and "This fell flat." Remember those wide margins we suggested on the manuscript several chapters back? Use them now to jot down notes, insights, and ideas about those red and green highlighted areas of the sermon. The important information is not that this illustration fell flat but why it did.

For example, what was the problem with this illustration? Was it the content? Was it the delivery? Was it the placement of the illustration? What could have strengthened the use of this illustration at this point? And yes, go ahead and ask yourself the tough questions: "Was this a solid illustration of what I was trying to say? Did this illustration even belong in this sermon? Why or why not?" Again, many of us preachers tend to fall in love with a neat story and can't wait to use it in a sermon whether it fits or not. This rigorous self-evaluation is the time and place to lose our infatuation with the story and to determine objectively if it fit or not.

Go through the manuscript several times with those highlighters, being tough but honest with yourself. Consider both the content of the sermon and the delivery. Critique your use of movement, gestures, vocal inflection, speed of delivery, pauses—all of it. Jot down many notes in those margins; use extra sheets of paper, if necessary. Jot down how a statement could have been written differently and more effectively, how a gesture could have been carried out to greater effect, how a vocal inflection could have strengthened a subpoint. In many ways, your notes on this sermon will become your textbook (or part of your continuing textbook) on preaching. (Yes, serious evaluation of a sermon is as tough as writing that sermon in the first place, but it is the way preachers learn to improve their effectiveness at proclaiming the good news.)

Next, dig out the profile of the congregation. You prepared this profile after the conversation with people from the congregation during your sermon preparation time. (We talked about the profile in Chapter 6.) Read over that profile in detail and, just as you did with the sermon manuscript, make notes on the profile. How accurate was your initial profile and your experience with the congregation? How would you change the profile, now that you've worshiped with the congregation and met many of the members of the congregation face to face? If your initial profile was not too accurate, don't blame the people with whom you spoke about the congregation. And don't blame yourself for misunderstanding and misinterpreting the nature of what you were told. It's not often that the initial profile of a congregation and the after-the-sermon profile of a congregation match. Profiling a congregation is difficult to do, but it is essential to effective preaching.

Why deal with this profile now that the sermon is completed? The basic reason is so that you can discover and rediscover the necessity of gearing a sermon to a particular congregation and the importance of knowing as much about that congregation as possible. One possible outcome is that you may have identified problems with an illustration or two. But was the problem with the illustration in general, or was the problem with the illustration in this particular congregation?

An example from a sermon I heard just this week: A young pastor friend of mine was preaching a weekday noontime sermon during a series of Lenten worship services at a large church. My friend is an avid sports fan, and this week is the week of the finals of the NCAA (National Collegiate Athletic Association) basketball tournament. My friend used several illustrations from the world of basketball tournaments to illustrate and illuminate his sermon's points. But these illustrations fell somewhat flat because the congregation that day consisted mostly of elderly women, many of whom had little knowledge of or interest in basketball tournaments. Get the point? They were good illustrations, but they were less appropriate in this setting than in other settings. Don't scrap the illustrations, but be careful about where and with whom you use them in the sermon.

Evaluation by Them

I really think you have to do your own evaluation before you ask others to evaluate your sermon. You may change your evaluation after hearing others speak of the sermon, but do your own evaluation first. Then comes what you've been waiting for: evaluation by other people.

So, who gives you feedback on the sermon? Beware of immediate family members, as they have to live with you. A spouse might say, "Great sermon." But rather than open up some issues, he or she might not go further than that. The same can be said of our children, even our grown children. The ties of family make honest evaluation difficult. This doesn't mean that we should not ask family members for some feedback, but it does suggest that we need some more objective evaluations than our immediate family can provide.

A good friend or two may be honest, open, and genuinely objective. Monday or even Tuesday is a good time to sit down with that friend (or friends) and to invite him or her to talk as honestly and openly as possible about the sermon. I've often invited a couple of friends to have dessert with me in a neutral setting, such as a favorite coffee shop. Quiz your friends about all dimensions of the sermon: content, delivery, illustrations, gestures, pauses, vocal inflections, the whole works. Ask them to comment on the invitation: Was it appropriate? Was the invitation tied to the main point of the sermon?

As you listen, feel free to ask questions for clarification, but don't—*do not*—get defensive or try to explain why you did or said something. Do the hardest thing we are ever asked to do: listen. Make notes, jot down ideas that come from what your friends are saying, press for specific details, seek both general reactions to the sermon as a whole and detailed reactions to elements within the sermon and its delivery.

Don't cut this evaluation session short; listen as long as your friends are commenting, be those comments positive or negative. Then, if you had coffee and dessert together, you pick up the check and thank your friends for their time and honesty. They have ministered to you in their forthrightness, and you will grow to become a more effective preacher as a result of honest feedback from those you trust.

If the church at which you preached tape records or videotapes the services of worship, ask for a copy of the service at which you preached. Critique your sermon on audio tape or videotape. But be prepared, as you will sound and appear far different from what you expect.

14

ROLL OUT THE BARREL?

Getting New Sermon Ideas

Congratulations. You've completed the cycle. You've conceived a sermon, written it, delivered it, and evaluated it. Ready to go again?

I was talking with a group of seminary students on one occasion, and one of them asked, "How can you do this every 168 hours?" I don't think I'd ever heard the question posed quite that way. But it is a fact that if you are going to serve as a pastor of a congregation, this cycle goes completely around every 168 hours. Few congregations are willing to accept hearing, "I just didn't have time to put a sermon together this week." So, yes, you go through this long, detailed, arduous cycle every single week if you are preaching on a regular basis.

Are there shortcuts? Are there steps that can be eliminated? The response to both of those queries is that there are none. If you are serious about preaching, about proclaiming the good news of the gospel (and if you are not serious, why have you read this far in this primer?), then you will not seek shortcuts or eliminate any steps. You will carefully go through this process in a regular, disciplined, careful way every week. Remember, we're not called United *Methodist* for nothing. That *Methodist* title was first a nickname of scorn for John Wesley and his friends at Oxford because Wesley and his fellow Christians were so methodical about their disciplines of faith. Preparing to preach is one of the most important disciplines you'll ever undertake, for the eternal souls of people hang in the balance.

Yes, go through this entire process every time you are called on to preach. No, it is not unrealistic. Yes, you do have the time. If you can't make the time to construct a sermon, politely decline the invitation to preach.

What Do I Do With the Sermon?

What do you do with the sermon you just labored so diligently to perfect and deliver, the sermon you critiqued so carefully, including all the marginal notes made before and after you delivered the sermon.

You file it. Start right now with a file of sermons. Use file folders, one for each sermon, and label each file folder prominently with four things:
• the title of the sermon;
• the Scripture texts on which the sermon is based;
• the date you preached the sermon;
• the place you preached the sermon.

Why these four? Because you'll need a cross-reference system. You may forget the title of a sermon but remember that it was preached in mid-October of last year. The date will save you here. Or you may remember preaching on a certain text several years ago. Or, perhaps as often as any other, you may remember the church where you preached. You'll discover that the more you preach, the more you need this cross-reference system.

But—and this is extremely important—do not file the sermon manuscript only. Include in that file folder the following:
1. the sermon manuscript;
2. the initial profile of the congregation to whom you preached this sermon;
3. the revised profile of the congregation to whom you preached this sermon;
4. the notes, the outline, or the cards you used to preach this sermon;
5. a copy of the worship bulletin from the church where you preached, if one is available (Go ahead and make notations on the worship bulletin: Did the hymns fit? Did all the components of the service work together? Was the service an integrated, unified service of worship and praise to God?);
6. any audio or video recording of that sermon. (OK. You can't file a videotape easily in a file folder. So, label the videotape with the same four items and start a file of video and audio tapes.)

Again, be sure to save and file the profile of the congregation. You want to know not only what you said but to whom you said it.

Why File?

You might be thinking that the reason for filing sermons is easy: You can preach them again. Not quite.

An old cliché says that you cannot make a soufflé rise twice. And you cannot preach a sermon in a second location and expect it to be as effective as it was the first time you preached it. If you do preach it twice, you'll wonder why it didn't fly as well as it did the first time.

Some great preachers have preached the same sermon over and over again, and that sermon just seems to get better and better. But you and I are not in that great preacher category yet, since we lack the years and years of experience writing and delivering sermons that those great preachers have. We have not had the successes they have had; and, more important, if we're just starting out, we haven't had the failures they have had. Don't let anyone fool you: Preaching is hard, tough, often discouraging work. And even the most famous preachers in the land will tell you countless stories of sermons over which they labored diligently that just did not fly, sermons in which, despite their best efforts, the good news of the gospel was simply not proclaimed. Even the apostle Paul met with what we'd call failure when he preached in Athens (Acts 17:16-34).

Why keep old sermons and the profiles of the congregations in which these sermons were preached? Because those old sermons are filled with your labor and effort, and a significant part of the labor and effort in them is in the marginal notes you made before and after delivering that sermon. You can learn a great deal about sermon construction, sermon delivery, and every other dimension of lifting up Christ from the pulpit by studying your old sermons and the notes you made about them.

If you are not preaching on a regular weekly basis, I'd urge you to review the last three or four sermons you preached every time you receive an invitation to preach. Do this before you begin your sermon writing and again after the sermon manuscript is complete. What worked well in those last three or four sermons? Did certain gestures, vocal inflections, and other elements of delivery seem to be well received? If so, how can you incorporate these into this current sermon legitimately?

On the other hand, what kinds of illustrations just didn't do a thing to support your proclamation of the gospel? Was the problem the content of the illustration, the way the illustration was related, or the positioning of the illustration? Figure it out and answer those questions, for they will help you avoid the same kinds of mistakes this time.

Or let's say that in your last several sermons you left the major, central point of the sermon until about two thirds of the way through the sermon. Something seemed to be lacking in each of those sermons, and, on reflection, this may be it.

Maybe in this sermon you're working on now, you'll want to make the major point earlier in the sermon. Studying our old sermons and the copious notes we made about them will help us try new ways and new forms of proclaiming the gospel in order to make that proclamation more effective. We learn from anything and everything in order to proclaim the good news of the gospel.

That Lection Again

People who preach occasionally may find themselves in a situation in which regular preachers often find themselves. Our lectionary is a three-year lectionary, meaning that the same lections or Scripture passages come around every three years. Some lections roll around every year and present the same problem in a slightly more intense way. For example, every year has an Ascension Sunday, a Trinity Sunday, a Transfiguration Sunday, to name a few on the Christian calendar. Several other Sundays are highlighted on our calendars every year and seem to beg for the same kind of message. Consider Aldersgate Sunday, Reformation Sunday, Mother's Day and Father's Day, the Sunday closest to the 4th of July, and the Sunday preceding Thanksgiving. What do you do if you preached one of these Sundays in the past and have in your file the sermon manuscript you used last time?

Much as you'd like to ignore these special days, you can't. Your sermon is going to have to deal with the special day somehow. A friend of mine recently told me that he just couldn't preach another Palm Sunday sermon, so on the last Sunday of Lent he preached on the text "Remember Lot's wife" (Luke 17:32). I don't know if and how he worked Palm Sunday into that—I suspect he didn't—but I also wonder if some of his people wanted the Palm Sunday–Passion Sunday experience and perhaps did not receive it.

The second option is to pull out that old sermon and preach it again. Why not? It worked last year (or three years ago); maybe it will work again now.

That old sermon will probably not work again this year. The main reason it may not work is that you're preaching it to an entirely different congregation, even if you've been preaching regularly in that church since last year or even long before that. Congregations are living, vital organisms that change in shape almost every week. Therefore, what worked well last year or three years ago worked because it fit the congregation of that time. But that does not mean it will fit the congregation this time, since the congregation is different.

If you doubt that, and if you've been preaching regularly in a congregation for a year or more, write down how the congregation has changed in that year: Who is coming to church now who wasn't attending worship then? Who is no longer attending worship, regardless of the reasons why this is so?

A third choice is reworking, adapting, or (as some say) tinkering with that sermon to make it work this year. A word to the wise: Tinkering with a sermon seldom makes that sermon better, but it does make that sermon sound like something with which someone has been tinkering. Maybe you can pick up some subpoints, maybe even the main point, perhaps even some illustrations, but a new Sunday demands a new sermon.

So, your best option is to buckle down and write a new outline and a new sermon. Do even more study this time around. Read more commentaries; find more angles on the text; look at the text from another perspective. Or, to use the popular language of today, think outside the box. Take Transfiguration Sunday, for example: You focused last year on the transfigured Jesus. This year look at the event through the eyes of Peter, James, and John. Or focus more on the ways in which the apostles were changed as they left the mountaintop for the valleys of suffering. The glory of the Scriptures is that they are ever new and ever lend themselves to new and different interpretations.

By now you should have gotten the point; we've used the approach of telling you what we're going to tell you, telling you, and then telling you what we've told you. The point is to not recycle sermons. Don't try to make an old sermon fit a new situation. Don't attempt to preach a sermon a second time (unless, of course, you are preaching several places or times on the same Sunday morning. And even then the sermon may need to be slightly different for each congregation.).

Leftover sermons do not warm up well, so don't try it.

Other People's Leftovers

The same goes for trying to preach someone else's sermon. You may have heard or read a brilliant sermon, but don't try to preach it yourself. Again, your situation is different from the original situation in which that sermon was preached. You are not the person who first conceived, wrote, and preached that sermon. And that sermon is not the result of your prayers, your study, your efforts, and, again, your prayers.

Yes, I know magazines and the Internet are filled with sermons on every conceivable subject, including the lectionary. And reading those sermons reveals that many of them are solid sermons based soundly on the Scriptures. Perhaps you can gather some ideas from magazines, journals, and the Internet. But do not simply pick up an Internet or journal sermon, no matter how great you think it is, and preach it as if it were your own.

Perhaps once in a great while—and then only rarely—you may want to preach a sermon written by someone else. You may have discovered it in a classic book of sermons, in a prominent journal, or somewhere else. If you are tempted to do so, do the following first:

Pray long and hard about using a prepackaged sermon. Then write down all the reasons why you should deliver this particular sermon to this particular congregation at this particular time. Notice here that the focus of these questions is not on the content or the brilliance of the sermon. The focus of these questions is on the situation in which you will be preaching. What is there about the situation—time, place, profile of congregation, and all the other factors—that commends using this sermon you found here and now? Be ruthless and honest. Not having time to go through the sermon-writing process is no answer.

If, after prayerful and careful thought and analysis of the congregation and the timing, you are still convinced that the most effective way you can proclaim the good news to these people at this time is through using a sermon you found in a book or on the Internet, then you must do these things:

- Read the sermon from the pulpit with an obvious manuscript in hand. Yes, I know, several chapters back we suggested not reading sermons verbatim. But this situation is different. You are presenting someone else's work, and that requires you to represent the person who wrote that sermon with complete accuracy. Reading the sermon is the only way you can do this.
- Introduce the sermon by indicating that you are going to read someone else's sermon; then tell the congregation the reasons you are doing so.
- Give full and complete identification of the writer of the sermon before you begin to read. Also give the source of the sermon. "I am reading a sermon titled 'Not My Will, But Thine,' written by the Rev. John Smith. This sermon first appeared in the March issue of *I'm a Preacher*. This publication grants blanket permission to use its contents in services of worship. The Rev. Mr. Smith writes..."

Did you catch a point in that sample statement? You're right; unless a magazine, journal, or book grants permission in writing for those materials to be used in services of worship, you are stealing someone else's property. No, *stealing* is not too strong a word, for that is what you are doing. If you are intent on using a sermon from a source that does not grant such blanket permission, you can contact the copyright holder in writing and request that permission be granted for you to use that sermon. That permission must be *in writing* and must be in hand before you preach that sermon. I cannot stress this too much: Anything less is plagiarism, which is a nice word for stealing the property of another. Don't do it, as it is not only illegal but also immoral and a violation of all that preachers are to uphold.

As you read the sermon, hold the manuscript so that all can see it; do not pretend to be preaching off notes or cards. You are reading a sermon. Each time you come to a major shift in emphasis or a subpoint and its accompanying paragraphs again give credit to the original author. This can be a simple, "The Rev. Mr. Smith continues," "I continue to read the Rev. Mr. Smith's sermon," or a similar kind of statement.

Do the same thing as the sermon ends. Again, make a simple statement, such as, "This concludes the Rev. Smith's sermon."

See what you're doing? You're making your congregation aware in several different ways that you are preaching someone else's sermon. In no way are you trying to claim this message as your own. You are using another's sermon with integrity.

What About Illustrations and Such?

Preachers are homiletical packrats. No preacher has yet lived and preached who did not borrow ideas, illustrations, and even points from the work of others. Each of us does it over and over again.

But again, basic morality demands that we credit the sources of our ideas, points, or illustrations. These credit lines within our sermons need not be labored, but we do have a responsibility to indicate our sources. "Did you read that story about the girl and her kitten in yesterday's *City Paper*?" "As Ishmael in Melville's *Moby Dick* asks on one occasion, 'What [is this] weighed...in the scales of the New Testament?'"

In Summary...

By far the best course of action is to prepare a new sermon for each new occasion of preaching. A sermon is more than the words on the paper. It is the effort you have put into it. It is the prayers you have offered over it and about it. It is the ability and the opportunity God has given you to proclaim the good news of the gospel.

Each time you stand behind the pulpit is a new time, an original time. The congregation is different; you are different; the message, although two thousand years old, is being presented in a fresh, new, and exciting way to a group of listeners who have never heard it presented in quite this way. That's why original sermons, based on prayer, study, and all the learnings from past sermons, convey the gospel as nothing else can.

Thanks be to God!

15

PREACHING ON SPECIAL OCCASIONS

Funerals, Weddings, Baptisms, and Other Special Occasions

As a preacher, one who is known to proclaim the gospel of Jesus Christ with power and conviction, you will be asked to speak and preach on many different kinds of occasions and in many different situations. In this brief chapter, we'll look at some of those occasions and make some comments that you might find helpful.

Will You Bring a Devotion?

One of the most frequent requests you'll receive is the invitation to do a devotional or a meditation in a small-group setting. Quite likely, you've already done a number of these, and it was that experience that led you to your interest in preaching.

A *devotional* is the words spoken at the beginning of a meeting, before a Sunday school class, or in some other situation. Often, those who ask you to bring a devotional (or whatever name they call it) are not clear about what they want. They think that some recognition of our Christian faith and of the lordship of Christ needs to be lifted up prior to the meeting, and you are the one to do it. Consequently, devotionals are sometimes toss-offs; that is, not carefully considered and delivered.

But the invitation to you to bring a devotional can be a great opportunity for you to glorify Christ and to proclaim the good news. Take each such invitation seriously, for you may be speaking to someone who needs the word of God in a special way at this time and may not even realize it.

Many of the suggestions for preparing a sermon are applicable for preparing a devotional for a special group or situation. Learn and know as much as possible about the group for whom you will be offering a devotional. Just as you develop a profile of a congregation before you preach, get as much information as you can about the organization or group to whom you will be speaking. A profile of a congregation describes the people in the congregation; a profile of those for whom you will be offering a devotional also includes something about the organization or the meeting that brings these people together. If you are preparing a devotional for a meeting of the United Methodist Women in your congregation, you might want to focus on one of the stories of strong women in the Bible, rather than, as a ridiculous example, the calling of the boy Samuel. Another example: I've been asked to speak to a group of hospital volunteers next week. I haven't written the devotional yet, but my comments will probably not focus as much on the need to get out and do more as they will focus on a sense of thanksgiving for those who are seeking to follow Christ's injunction to love one another.

Another example: I once heard a young man present a powerful devotional on Christian grief counseling in nursing homes. His points were solid, well conceived, and well presented, but he was speaking to a gathering of Christian preschool teachers and teacher's aides. If he made a connection between what his listeners were doing (and the reason for which they were gathered) and his message, I didn't get it.

One of the things that many people like the least about a meeting or organization opening devotional is that some people who are invited to present devotionals get carried away and preach thirty-minute sermons. In a word, don't. The whole idea of a devotional is that it is short, concise, and to the point. It makes one point, and one point only. It does not have a lengthy introduction; it does not have a lot of stories and illustrations; it does not include the approach of telling them what you're going to tell them, telling them, and then telling them what you've told them. Indeed, a devotional may be one simple story, the object of which is so clear that you need not explain or illuminate it. Want some good examples of what I'm describing here? Read some of Jesus' parables, which are short, precise, to the point, and thought provoking. That's the best kind of devotional.

But the fact that a devotional is short, precise, and to the point means that a devotional, if it is to be effective, requires a lot of planning and careful preparation. Any experienced preacher or public speaker will tell you that it's easier to make a point in a thousand words than it is in a hundred words. Please don't toss off these opportunities to present devotionals. Give them careful attention; write full manuscripts; use outlines or note cards; proclaim the good news of the gospel in five, rather than in twenty, minutes.

Ground your devotional, whatever it is, in the Scriptures. Regardless of the organization, the meeting, or the situation, we are called on to be scriptural preachers and speakers. Even if you are building your devotional around a story, be sure to anchor it in the Scriptures.

And one more comment about offering a devotional before a meeting of a committee or organization, either within or beyond your congregation: If appropriate, remain for the duration of the meeting. Don't drop by just to do a quick devotional, for it shows a lack of respect for the committee or organization for which you are offering a devotional. By helping these people focus for a moment on God, you are becoming one with these people, if only for an hour or so.

On some occasions, you may be invited to present a devotional in a secular situation. In one small community in which I pastored, I was asked several times to bring devotionals to city council meetings. When invited to do such a devotional, be clear that you come representing the Christian faith and that your devotional will lift up Jesus Christ and proclaim the good news of the gospel. Do not be ashamed of the gospel, and avoid watering down the gospel for fear of offending someone in a secular setting. If the person who invites you to make opening remarks shows some hesitancy about your commitment to proclaim the faith, it is better to withdraw than to compromise.

Would You Say Something at the Funeral?

Another situation in which lay speakers often find themselves is being invited to say something at the funeral of a friend or relative. Recognize that you are being invited not just because you are a lay speaker and have a growing reputation for your ability to preach but because you know the person who has died or the family. In short, you are being invited because you are a friend, not because you are a preacher. In all likelihood, a clergyperson will conduct the actual funeral, and you will be invited to speak briefly within the funeral service.

How do you prepare? Pull out *The United Methodist Book of Worship* (your copy should be well-marked and somewhat dog-eared by now) and turn to "Services of Death and Resurrection." As so often with *The Book of Worship*, the rubrics (the materials printed in red type) provide a great storehouse of information about the rites and ceremonies of the church. Study those rubrics carefully (pages 139 to 141 and throughout the services themselves) and get the flow of the service of death and resurrection firmly in mind. A funeral is a service of worship, and everything must be carried out in a most worshipful manner.

Next, get with the presiding clergyperson. If that person is a United Methodist, great. You're both coming from the same understanding of a service of death and resurrection. If that person is from another denomination, ask for a copy, even a rough copy, of the order of service that will be used in the funeral service.

Find out what part the presiding clergyperson would like you to take. This may be a Scripture reading, a prayer, a reading of the obituary (common in some parts of the country), or, most often, a few words about the person who has died. You have been invited because you are a friend, not because you are a preacher.

Again, brevity and precision are keys here. Personal reminiscences are appropriate if they are brief and to the point. If these can be tied with integrity to a Scripture passage or a promise from the Scriptures, do so.

But remember, regardless of your personal pulpit style, a funeral is not the place for overly dramatic gestures or vocal inflections; it is not the place for histrionics (regardless of what the presiding clergyperson might do). A funeral is a setting in which all stand before the mystery of death and the promise of the resurrection; therefore, the speaker's deportment must reflect genuine respect and a sense of awe before these mysteries that we cannot fully comprehend. In view of this, your comments must be totally honest. If the one who has died was not a saint, do not picture her or him as being so. But at the same time, this is not in any sense the time to point out her or his faults. Remember what we taught our children? "If you can't say something nice, don't say anything at all." But you can always say something nice in terms of God's promises to calm, console, and claim.

The same goes when you are invited to speak at the funeral of someone you do not know. Often, funeral directors will invite lay speakers to conduct the funerals of people with no church affiliation whatsoever. If you find yourself in that situation, attend the visiting hours (the wake, or whatever name is used in your region of the country) and informally pick up as much information about the deceased as you can. Work some of this into your comments, but emphasize that each person is a child of God, loved by God, and claimed by God.

A Few Other Occasions

Sometimes lay speakers are asked to say a few words at the wedding of a close friend or, more often, a relative. Again, use *The United Methodist Book of Worship* to learn as much as you can about conducting weddings. Pay specific attention to the rubrics, the material printed in red type. Be comfortable in your own head about the various components of a service of worship that commemorates a wedding. That's right: A wedding is a service of worship in which God's blessing is invoked on the union of a woman and a man. A wedding is not just a prelude to a huge reception; it is and must be the most important element on the wedding day.

As you did with the funeral, spend some time with the presiding clergyperson. Go over the wedding service with her or him, and be clear on what you are to do (and not to do). The presiding clergyperson—not the florist, one of the mothers, or someone's great aunt—is in charge of the wedding, for a wedding is a holy and sacred rite and needs to be treated as such.

What do you say if you are asked to say something at a wedding? Again, ground your comments in Scripture. See page 119 in *The United Methodist Book of Worship* for appropriate Scriptures on which to base a wedding meditation. For example, I Corinthians 13 and Colossians 3:12-17 are perhaps the most often used texts and lend themselves to a brief, simple, direct meditation on the nature of Christian love between wife and husband.

> **Caution:** Do not use Ruth 1:16-17 in a wedding service. This would be a misuse of this text, for this text has nothing to do with marriage or with wives and husbands. Yes, I know it's popular both in song and meditation at marriages, but to use this text in such a setting is to misunderstand, misinterpret, and misuse the Scriptures. Why compromise the integrity of the Scriptures when passages such as those in *The United Methodist Book of Worship* are appropriate?

Again, the comments made about devotionals at secular functions hold for comments at weddings. Do not apologize for a Christian perspective, but help the wedding couple comprehend that their love is grounded in God's love for them through Jesus Christ. If they are uncomfortable with this, perhaps you ought not to speak.

A close friend of mine was asked to officiate at the wedding of a Christian and a non-Christian a few years ago. The non-Christian asked that all references to anything Christian be excluded from the wedding ceremony. The obvious question: Then why be married in a Christian church? My friend politely suggested that this couple be married in a civil ceremony. I would agree.

All of the comments about devotionals and funerals are precisely on target with weddings also. Keep your comments brief and to the point. Brevity and precision are fundamental here; make each word count. That means you'll have to work doubly hard on the manuscript so that the wedding meditation is directly on target.

Here's a hint about comments both at weddings and at funerals: Often, the people most involved are so emotionally engaged that they do not hear exactly what you are saying. I'm speaking here of the couple being married or the immediate family of the deceased at a funeral. Many preachers and even those who are asked to say a few words polish their manuscripts, type them up in neat and final form, and give a nice copy of the comments to the marriage couple sometime after the wedding or to the immediate family after a funeral. You'll be surprised at how much this is appreciated.

As you preach more and more, you will be invited more and more to offer short devotions and meditations in various settings. Remember that each of these is a significant opportunity to proclaim the good news of Jesus Christ. Develop each meditation carefully and prayerfully; seek to proclaim the Word that the particular listeners need to hear. Remember, you are serving our Lord by seeking to make disciples, and God has called you to make disciples in this particular way.

~ ~ ~

Preaching—whether a three-minute meditation prior to a committee meeting or a full sermon before a congregation of hundreds of people—is a great honor and privilege that calls forth our humility, our obedience, and our best attention to the leading of God. Believe in your heart that you would not be reading this primer if you had not been called by God and equipped by God for this sacred task. So...

Go preach!

A BEGINNING PREACHER'S LIBRARY

Your library as a beginning preacher ought to include the following:

- **At least three translations of the Bible**
  1. A New Revised Standard Version study Bible (*The New Oxford Annotated Bible, The Cambridge Annotated Study Bible,* and *The HarperCollins Study Bible* are all excellent choices.)
  2. One modern translation (The American Bible Society's Contemporary English Version is an outstanding translation that is easy to read.)
  3. One other translation, preferably in a study Bible format (The New International Version study Bible is a good choice, as is the New King James Version.)

- **A concordance**
  Exhaustive concordances are huge and detailed but invaluable. In addition, you may want a smaller concordance. Perhaps the best buy in a less-than-exhaustive concordance is *The Concise Concordance to the New Revised Standard Version* (Oxford University Press).

- **At least two Bible dictionaries**
  (Don't bother with pocket or concise dictionaries; they are not worth your time or money.)
  The five-volume *Interpreter's Dictionary of the Bible* (Abingdon Press) is a first choice, but it is expensive. Select *Dictionary of the Bible* (Oxford University Press), *Holman Bible Dictionary* (Holman Bible Publishers), or the *HarperCollins Bible Dictionary* (Harper San Francisco).

- **A good Bible atlas**
  Excellent choices include *Oxford Bible Atlas* (Oxford University Press), *The Macmillan Bible Atlas* (Hungry Minds), and *The HarperCollins Concise Atlas of the Bible* (Harper San Francisco).

- **At least two (preferably three) good Bible commentaries**
  The *New Interpreter's Bible* (Abingdon Press) and the older *Interpreter's Bible* (Abingdon Press) are outstanding multivolume commentaries. *The Interpreter's One Volume Commentary on the Bible* (Abingdon Press) remains a fine choice, as

does *HarperCollins Bible Commentary* (Harper San Francisco). William Barclay's commentaries (Westminster John Knox Press) are popular and solid, as is the *Basic Bible Commentary* (Abingdon Press).

- A copy of the *Gospel Parallels* (Thomas Nelson Publishers).

- **A good history of Christianity**
  If you can afford it, spring for *The Oxford Illustrated History of Christianity* (Oxford University Press). But many good histories of the Christian church are available.

- **Your own copy of *The United Methodist Hymnal* and of *The United Methodist Book of Worship***
  Hint to family members: These make great gifts for lay speakers and beginning preachers.

- **A copy of *The New Handbook of the Christian Year*** (Abingdon Press).

- **A copy of *The HarperCollins Bible Pronunciation Guide*** (Harper San Francisco).

- **A good grammar reference book**
  The Harbrace College Handbook (Harcourt Brace & Company) has been around for years. It is continually updated and is still the best quick reference for grammar. Learn to use it, and use it diligently. Another book to help you improve your writing skills is *The Elements of Style,* by William Strunk, Jr., and E.B. White (Simon & Schuster).

- **A good, solid collegiate dictionary**
  Avoid small paperback dictionaries, since they are limited. A dictionary such as *The American Heritage Dictionary of the English Language* (Houghton Mifflin Co.) is an excellent choice.

- **A thesaurus**
  Many are available, such as *Roget's International Thesaurus* (HarperCollins). Choose a good, big one and then learn how to use it.

AN ILLUSTRATIVE BIBLIOGRAPHY ON PREACHING

Note that this is called an *illustrative* bibliography. That means it is intended to give you an idea of the breadth and range of materials available on the subject of preaching. You will discover as you browse bookstores and the Internet that books on preaching come in two forms: books about preaching and books of sermons. Start with books about preaching. Then, as you become more experienced, move to books of sermons.

The Art of Preaching Old Testament Narrative, by Steven D. Mathewson (Baker Book House, 2002).

Biblical Preaching: The Development and Delivery of Expository Messages, by Haddon W. Robinson (Baker Book House, 1999).

Finally Comes the Poet: Daring Speech for Proclamation, by Walter Brueggemann (Fortress Press, 1990).

Fundamentals of Preaching, by John Killinger (Fortress Press, 1996).

Handbook of Contemporary Preaching, edited by Michael Duduit (Baptist Sunday School Board, 1993).

Imagining a Sermon ("Abingdon Preacher's Library"), by Thomas H. Troeger (Abingdon Press, 1990).

Peculiar Speech: Preaching to the Baptized, by William H. Willimon (William B. Eerdmans, 1992).

The Practice of Preaching, by Paul Scott Wilson (Abingdon Press, 1998).

Preaching, by Fred B. Craddock (Abingdon Press, 1990).

Preaching the Topical Sermon, by Ronald J. Allen (Westminster John Knox Press, 1992).

Preaching to a Postmodern World: A Guide to Reaching Twenty-First Century Listeners, by Graham MacPherson Johnston (Baker Book House, 2001).

Telling the Truth: The Gospel as Tragedy, Comedy, and Fairy Tale, by Frederick Buechner (Harper San Francisco, 1985).

When God Is Silent: The 1997 Lyman Beecher Lectures on Preaching, by Barbara Brown Taylor (Cowley Publications, 1998).

Preaching is:

Teaching
Witnessing *
Expressing
Faith - Sharing *

" Making God's word Hearable "

To make things "hearable" find out a little about
* the congregation - there might be something
going on with them that needs a specific
message.

Ask Questions -